Strange People

BY FRANK EDWARDS

My First 10,000,000 Sponsors
Strangest of All
Stranger Than Science

FRANK EDWARDS

Author of "Stranger Than Science" Presents

STRANGE PEOPLE

Citadel Press / Secaucus, N.J.

Published by Citadel Press
A division of Lyle Stuart Inc.
120 Enterprise Ave., Secaucus, N.J. 07094
In Canada: Musson Book Company
A division of General Publishing Co. Limited
Don Mills, Ontario
Manufactured in the United States of America
ISBN 0-8065-1011-0

To Tommy Austin and Freddie Lee
my two fishing buddies

Table of Contents

PART THREE

Introduction

The innumerable instances of unexplained and unexplainable experiences which have befallen credible witnesses serve to emphasize the limitations of our understanding of the laws which govern the world about us.

The evidence which I submit to you in this book is only a small part of that which is available. It is my belief, arrived at after a long period of cautious consideration, that we must be surrounded by forces as yet unrecognized: That these forces cannot be weighed, registered or measured by instruments currently available to us, although it seems probable that we *are* affected by them, voluntarily or otherwise.

The accounts which I have gathered here seem to substantiate the words of Thomas Wolfe, who said:

"Beneath the tides of sleep and time
Strange fish are moving!"

They are, indeed!

Let's have a look at them.

FRANK EDWARDS

October, 1961

9

1

The Monkey Girl

The rain and wind that whipped the sideshow tent flaps had long since driven away the customers. Carl Lauther was ready to turn out the lights when he heard footsteps in the ooze and a dripping, bareheaded couple stepped inside the tent. The woman carried a blanket-wrapped bundle in her arms. She held it out to Lauther and said something in a foreign language which he did not understand.

With the caution which is second nature to people in the tent-show world, Lauther refused to touch the bundle until he knew what this was all about. He sent his wife to get a member of the show who spoke some French and Spanish and who understood a smattering of Portuguese.

With the help of this interpreter, the couple was finally able to tell them that they had brought a baby that was "different" — a magnificent understatement. When the mother pulled back the blankets, Lauther realized that he was looking at the freak find of the century—a baby girl covered from head to foot with long, silky, black hair.

Lauther got in touch with his attorneys and the necessary adoption requirements were carefully fulfilled. Then the parents left the show and never came back. They had ridded themselves of their freak and that was all they were interested in.

The Lauthers were very fond of their strange charge and Priscilla loved them in return. They gave her a chimpanzee for a playmate and, when she was old enough to exhibit, Priscilla played to standing-room crowds as "the monkey girl who lives with apes." It was as though the fantastic Tarzan stories had suddenly come to life.

Priscilla had come to the Lauthers in 1929. By 1946 she was a well-developed woman and one of the best known attractions in the outdoor show world. She was intelligent and she was healthy, except for a dental problem—she had two sets of teeth, one row behind the other, and she needed extensive and expensive surgery to correct it. Her foster parents simply did not have the money, because of several financial reverses, and they were in a quandary.

At that point a wealthy and eccentric woman who raised giant apes as a sort of hobby entered the picture. If Priscilla would go with her, she said, she would gladly finance the surgery. The Lauthers were reluctant to let her go, yet they did not want to retain her when the girl needed the very help this strange woman offered.

Priscilla, "the monkey girl who lives with apes," was torn between love and necessity and was just about to go with the odd benefactress when, somehow, word reached the girl that the woman wanted to experiment with her in a cross-breeding with her pet apes. Priscilla balked.

She stayed with the sideshow, married a young freak who had a skin ailment which caused him to be exhibited as "The Alligator Boy" and they were then exhibited as "The World's Strangest Couple"—which was hardly an exaggeration. The money poured in, Priscilla financed her own dental operation, and she and her husband enjoyed a happy married life such as few freaks ever know.

The condition in which the body is covered with hair is known in medical terminology as hirsuteness. Probably the best known case was that of the young man whom Barnum exhibited as "Jo-Jo, The Dog-Faced Boy." Photographs of him show that his entire face, including even the forehead and ears, was thickly covered with long silky hair which he kept cut and brushed so that he did, as Barnum claimed, look like a well-groomed Skye terrier. Medics who examined him at the suggestion of the canny showman reported that Jo-Jo was covered from head to foot with this long, wavy brown hair, just as Priscilla was so many years later.

2

Giants And Midgets

Showmen are always on the lookout for those strange people who can be exhibited as freaks. Often the subjects' families will write to the shows and invite inspection; for many of these freaks are burdens to their relatives. And, too, many freaks support parasitic relatives who have sold or given them to side show operators with that very result in mind.

For years the noted midget exhibited as Tom Thumb made a living for his entire family. Later, after he had become world-famous, he discontinued this practice, saved his money and died a wealthy man. But Tom, in real life Charles Stratton, was an exception not only in that he was so diminutive, but also, in belatedly taking over control of his own affairs and making a success of the venture. Few sideshow freaks can say as much.

Another little man who left a lasting impression was the renowned Geoffrey Hudson. When he was eight years old and slightly less than fourteen inches in height, he was presented at the table of Charles I in a pie. At the age of thirty he measured exactly eighteen inches in height. The Queen, who was very fond of him, sent Geoffrey to France to secure a midwife for her impending accouchement, and, while he was there, Hudson was insulted by an official who had the ill-grace to ridicule the midget's diminutive proportions. Geoffrey challenged the detractor to a duel and brought him down with one shot.

This courageous little chap is probably best known for still another duel which he fought in England, a battle to the death with a turkey gobbler which had "insulted" him by stealing his lunch. The bird outweighed him by several pounds and towered well above him, but Geoffrey finally slew his adversary, and, by way of celebrating the victory, Hudson and his friends ate the loser.

Doctors tell us that giants and midgets result from the malfunctioning of the pituitary gland, located deep in the brain. Too little pituitary extract and the result is a miniature human; too much, and we have a giant. There was a time, however, when these extremes of abnormality were viewed with awe, for it was felt that they had been especially designated as favorites of the gods. Kings and emperors surrounded themselves with midgets and dwarfs for good luck and gaiety; with giants for protection.

Giants have fascinated people and dominated folk tales since the dawn of history. The Bible tells of Goliath, who towered somewhere above nine feet and who amused himself by tossing cabbage-sized boulders into the ranks of his enemies. His downfall at the hands of David is a lesson in strategy, a demonstration that, by outsmarting the more powerful enemy, it is possible to overcome him.

In addition to Goliath of Gath, ancient records also mention Orestes. The Greeks who measured him for burial said he was slightly more than ten feet tall and of tremendous bulk.

During the reign of Augustus Caesar, workmen in the garden of Sallustia came upon two huge tombs cut side by side in the rock and carefully concealed. Examination revealed that they contained the remains of the noted giants, Secundilla and Posio, who were almost ten feet tall and to whom the task of guarding the renowned gardens had been assigned. Their widely-publicized ferocity and awesome proportions were very effective in keeping trespassers and thieves away. When they died, their bodies were hidden and news of their passing was suppressed, while their evil reputations carried on their work for years.

According to Josephus, the ancient historian, among the hostages sent by the King of Persia to Rome was a prize specimen named Eleazar. Eleazar, a Jewish giant, was nearly eleven feet tall. He was not unusually strong or heavy, however; but at the dining table he was a magnificent trencherman. The Romans matched him against some prodigious eaters and Eleazar always won the bets for them.

History records that in the twelfth century, King Eugene of Scotland had brought before him a native giant who stood eleven feet six inches tall. The monster was pale and sickly so the King ordered him away lest he spread his ailment among the residents of the castle.

Most giants reach their extraordinary height because of the unusual development of their leg bones. As a general rule, giants are not physically strong. A notable exception to this rule was the famed Angus McAskill, who exhibited for a time under the banner of Phineas Barnum.

McAskill was born in Scotland in 1825 and came to Nova Scotia when he was a small boy. There was nothing unusual about him until he reached his teens and then he began to grow at a remarkable rate.

By the time he was twenty-one years of age Angus McAskill was seven-feet-nine and weighed three hundred and eighty pounds. Doctors who measured him in New York City in 1845 reported that he had a seventy-inch chest and weighed four hundred and five pounds "none of it fat."

Barnum hired him and Angus McAskill toured many lands, amazing the spectators with his feats of strength, which included lifting objects that weighed up to fifteen hundred pounds. As a finale to the act, McAskill held a wooden platter in his hand while Tom Thumb danced a jig on the platter.

When a professional prize fighter finally goaded him into a ring battle, McAskill brought it to a quick termination by simply crushing his opponent's hand in his own.

But there were limits beyond which even he could not go, and his career came to a sudden end when McAskill made a thousand-dollar bet that he could lift, with his bare hands, a twenty-two-hundred pound ship's anchor. After a terrible struggle he did it; but, in trying to let the anchor back to earth, he injured his shoulder and spine. Wealthy, McAskill retired to his home in Nova Scotia, where he died in 1863.

One of the best known giants of Europe was the celebrated Charles O'Brien—the Irish Giant. He also wrote his name O'Byrne and O'Bryne, which makes for confusion in tracing his story, but they are all the same giant, as researchers eventually discover.

He was born in 1761, attained his full growth by the

17

time he was seventeen, when he stood eight feet, four inches tall. Showmen vied with each other for his services and O'Brien soon found he was making a nice living by simply being himself.

It was an Eden into which the serpent soon appeared in the form of Dr. John Hunter, an indefatigable fellow who longed to possess the skeleton of this altitudinous Irishman. He broached the subject to O'Brien, who was understandably shocked. Dr. Hunter vowed that he *would* have the giant's bones and O'Brien spent his few remaining years trying to prevent Hunter from carrying out his threat.

Harried by Hunter or his agents, O'Brien had no peace. In 1783 he became ill and realized that he could not live much longer; so he entered into an agreement with some fishermen to take his body out into the Irish Channel, weight it heavily with lead, and sink it into deep water. A few weeks later the giant learned that Dr. Hunter had bribed the fishermen to deliver the body to him. The harassed giant had to make other arrangements.

His life savings had been stolen from him during his illness and, as he shuffled out onto the stage for his appearances, O'Brien saw in the crowds the face of his tormentor, come vulture-like to await the end. It is small wonder that the giant died of a nervous breakdown.

A group of his friends had sworn to protect his corpse and they dutifully stood guard over his grave. But theirs was a hollow gesture, for Dr. Hunter had bribed the undertaker to switch coffins on the mourners. The one they buried was full of stones. O'Brien's corpse went into the doctor's possession and, as a result, the skeleton of the famed Irish Giant stands today in the Museum of the Royal College of Surgeons in Dublin.

At Manistee, Michigan, on the very sultry afternoon of July 15, 1940, there passed away a most remarkable young man named Robert Wadlow. This gentle giant was twenty-two years old, weighed four hundred ninety-three pounds and was eight feet, ten-and-a-half inches tall at the time of his death. He wore heavy metal braces on one foot and it was an infection due to friction from this brace that caused his untimely end. He was the tallest man in modern medical records.

3

Fat Men

The title of world's heaviest human is lost in controversy. Although the ancients made much of midgets, dwarfs, and giants, they seldom mentioned weight unless it was that of a giant of exceptional strength. The fat people of circuses and carnivals, in spite of the fantastic claims made for them, seldom exceed five hundred pounds in actual tonnage. They dress in loose-fitting garments to enhance their billowing blubber and are often exhibited alongside dwarfs or midgets for added contrast.

Robert Earl Hughes, who died on July 11, 1958, in Bremen, Indiana, was a circus fat man who claimed that he weighed fifteen hundred pounds. It is a fact that he was so big that he could not be moved from his trailer to the hospital. After death his body had to be lifted from his specially-built bed by the type of crane used for handling wrecked automobiles. His actual weight at time of death turned out to be one thousand and forty-one pounds, which is impressive, but not a record.

Probably the heaviest human on record in this country was Johnny Alee, who lived out his short span in the little crossroad community of Carbon, North Carolina.

He was born in 1853 and was chunky, but not exceptionally so, until he reached the age of ten. Then Johnny developed a ravenous appetite and began to accumulate fat so rapidly that by the time he was fifteen he could scarcely support his own weight, and he could no longer get out the front door of the house. His thighs were so well padded that grown men could scarcely reach around one of them.

Johnny could walk only with the greatest effort. A trip from the huge chair in which he sat to the table fifteen feet away was a major expedition which took fifteen minutes and plenty of assistance. It was a struggle both ways, and left him exhausted.

His weight was the indirect cause of his death in 1887 at the age of thirty-three.

Johnny lived in a house built on the side of a hill and this left the parlor suspended about eight feet above the ground, on thick log stilts. One day as he eased his eleven hundred and thirty-two pounds across the floor to a point where he could peek out the parlor door, the flooring gave way and he plunged through to his armpits. There he dangled helplessly while neighbors worked frantically to rig a block and tackle to pull him back to safety. Suddenly they noticed that his labored breathing had ceased. The doctors who later weighed him on the coal-office scales decided that Johnny Alee had died of heart failure induced by fear of falling six feet to the earth which his feet had not touched in nineteen years.

4

Two Headed Children

Other outrageous pranks that nature plays include such hapless creatures as the two-headed baby born at Petersburg, Indiana, on December 12, 1953. The twins lived several weeks. One head seemed "normal" but the other, while it could work its mouth and eyes, showed no signs of developing intelligence. The bodies shared a common spine but the heads moved about, slept and ate, independently of each other.

In Tipton County, Indiana, on June 24, 1889, was born the monstrosity known in medical annals as the "Jones Twins"—one trunk, with heads on opposite ends of it, the four legs jammed together, the arms placed normally. They were exhibited publicly for more than a year and died in February of 1891 at St. John's Hotel in Buffalo, New York.

In 1961, a circus freak lived in Miami who had three legs, the extra member projecting from the spine just above the sacrum and having sufficient strength to support the man, tripod fashion, when he spent the winter fishing from the highway bridges. Needless to say, he stopped traffic.

A Dr. Wells, writing in the *American Journal of Obstetrics* in 1888, reported that one of his patients was a twenty-year-old girl who had four well-formed legs, the outside pair being stronger and longer to such an extent that she used them for walking. She was still alive and in good health, Wells reported, when he treated her in 1891, at which time she was pregnant.

In May of 1829, a thirty-two-year-old woman in Sassari, Sardinia, gave birth to a monster with two heads. They were joined by individual spines to the abdomen of a female, so the parents called the creature, Ritta-Christina. The two heads showed considerable differences in likes and dislikes, eating, sleeping and crying at different times.

The poverty-stricken parents made their way to Paris, where they eked out an existence by showing the incredible baby; but authorities forced the exhibition to stop on the contention that it was "degrading." With no income, the baby soon died of cold and exposure in its unheated room. Fortunately some medics managed to prevent authorities from burning the body, as they intended, and it was subjected to an autopsy which showed that the two heads used a common heart and stomach. The curious little skeleton is still on view in Paris.

5

The Scottish Brothers

The Court of James III of Scotland was enlivened by one of the best known freaks in history, the so-called "Scottish Brothers." Like the hapless case of the two-headed girls mentioned previously, their bodies merged into a common abdomen, with one set of genitals and two normal legs. The King had them sent to him for safekeeping and education, which included musical training, foreign languages and painting. The brothers had strong likes and dislikes in these various fields and, as they become very proficient as linguists, painters and musicians they would often get into arguments and would even come to blows, their four arms flailing madly at each other, hampered somewhat by the adjoining arms getting in each other's way. It, or they, lived twenty-eight years, one brother dying five days before the other, who "moaned piteously as he crept about the castle gardens, carrying with him the dead body of the brother from whom only death could separate him and to whom death would again join him."

6

Strange Eyes

Anomalies of the eyes are rather more numerous than is generally recognized. In the *Boston Medical Journal* for 1854, an English authority named W. Drury is quoted on the four-eyed man of Cricklade, whom he examined. The man had two pairs of eyes, one pair above the other, and all brown, encircled with red around the enormously large pupils. Said Drury: "He could shut any eye independently of the others. He could also revolve each eye independently in its orbit or could turn them to look in different directions, which was most distracting to the onlooker." Mr. Drury did not like the four-eyed man because he used profanity and sang "in a screeching voice to which I could not listen without disgust."

For years, sideshow and circus men have tried to lure into their fold a true Cyclops who lives in a backwoods community in Mississippi. He is a Negro with a normal-sized eye in the center of his forehead. But he wants no part of show business and, having been pestered by so many showmen, he makes his resentment menacingly apparent when he spots one trying to make him an offer. The man is now (1961) middle-aged, and his life has been a long series of dodging implacable promoters who want to make him (and themselves) rich by exploiting his congenital oddity.

The only case of its kind was that of Edward Mordrake —scion of an aristocratic British family, who had a face on the back of his head. It had eyes, lips, nose and ears. It could see (that is, he could see through its eyes!). It could cry and laugh, but it could neither eat nor speak. Generally, it just leered and drooled. Little by little, the likable, intelligent young man who was cursed with this face behind his back—this devil twin—lost his mind and died a raving lunatic.

7

The Elephant Boy

What must have been one of the most frightening freaks in history was a tragic creature known as the Elephant Boy—the son of poverty-stricken parents who had sold the child to an itinerant showman to be rid of him. For an account of him, we have that set down by Sir Frederick Treves, a medical expert who was called to tend a "sick boy" on a bitter cold night in the 1870's. The doctor was led to a nearly barren room, where he was directed to a pile of rags in the corner. When he pulled back the rags, the eminent medic was admittedly staggered by what confronted him:

"He had a fleshy appendage hanging down from his forehead like an elephant's trunk. A spongy growth covered his neck. He was completely hairless. His forehead covered one eye. A mass of bone from the roof of his mouth projected out from his upper jaw. He had no nose. His body was hung with sacks of wrinkled skin. His right hand resembled a fin. His feet were too swollen to permit him to walk, except by a shuffling gait. In addition, he had been dropped when a baby and his spine was twisted out of shape."

27

Since the showman who owned the Elephant Boy could not get permission to exhibit the shocking creature, the two of them were penniless. Dr. Treves gave them enough money to get back to France, but a short time later the doctor found the youngster huddled in the gutter, whimpering, with a crowd picking at the crude garment he had pulled over his head to conceal his condition.

Sir Frederick Treves then took the boy to his own home where he could have him cared for and could examine him at leisure. When word spread that such an astonishing freak could be seen there, many notables came and saw, and left substantial tips to help care for the youngster. At length the boy was sent to a farm where he would no longer be badgered by the curious.

Due to his incredible deformity, the lad had always slept in a sitting position, with his great misshapen head on his knees, the pendulous flaps hanging on either side. Now that he had the means to live like other people he decided to sleep like them, on his back.

Alone in his room, over the stables, he laid down flat on his back, perhaps for the first time in his life, certainly for the last time. The massive head dangled over the end of the bed, closing the slender tube through which he breathed, and the most frightful freak on record died, as so many freaks have died, wishing that he could be like other people.

8

Little Lulu —
The Georgia Wonder

In the late summer of 1883 the little community of Cedartown, Tennessee, played host to a steadily growing swarm of visitors, all drawn by the desire to see for themselves the incredible feats attributed to fourteen-year-old Lulu Hurst, the shy, frail daughter of a local Baptist deacon. Reporters from the *Atlanta Constitution* and the *Rome Bulletin* came and marveled and wrote glowing accounts of "the wonderful Lulu Hurst" as they called her.

It was inevitable that she would have to give a public exhibition. Although her deeply religious parents were opposed, they saw in this move a means to ease the insistent demand to watch Lulu perform. So, reluctantly, they agreed to permit Lulu to appear publicly and a local hall in Cedartown was secured for the purpose.

It was September and it was hot. The hall was jammed with persons who had come from miles around. On the stage, brightly lit by a score of oil lamps, were a dozen guests of honor including judges, lawyers, doctors, bankers and members of the state legislature. Lulu's father was there to act as master of ceremonies.

A husky male volunteer from the audience was placed in the center of the stage and handed a folded umbrella. He grasped it firmly, one hand near the handle, the other near the top—and braced his feet, for he had been instructed to keep the umbrella from moving . . . if he could.

Lulu Hurst, who stood scarcely more than shoulder high to him, stepped up and placed the palm of her right hand against the umbrella. For a full minute, in a silence so deep that the swishing of the palm leaf fans was the only sound, the tableau continued. Then, as suddenly as though a demon had taken over, the man and the umbrella began to jerk up and down and to twist violently from side to side. Lulu still had only her open palm against the umbrella but the farmer who held it was clutching it with both hands. Man and umbrella darted from side to side across the stage.

The man had clearly lost control of the struggle. A final thrust swung him sidewise into the laps of the dignitaries on the stage and Lulu fell, gasping for breath.

The astounded audience was gasping, too, from sheer amazement. How could this slightly-built girl fling a grown man about the stage in spite of his best efforts?

Before they had time to recover from their astonishment, the second part of the performance was under way. Three members of the group on the stage braced their feet and held a common hickory cane tightly across their chests. Lulu placed the open palm of her left hand against the cane and a moment later the three men went tumbling backward, heels over head, to the uproarious delight of the audience.

The performance lasted for more than an hour and it consisted of variations on the theme of a young and slightly-built girl performing feats of strength that defied understanding. The audience, including the reporters, went out amazed and enthusiastic.

Instead of satisfying the demand for a demonstration of the young girl's powers, the resultant publicity multiplied the requests. As a natural consequence, Lulu Hurst was soon booked for public appearances in major cities all over the nation; and for two years she was one of the greatest attractions on the stage. No performer in the United States ever had a more meteoric career and few, if any, have been more sensational.

The puzzling sequence of events that led up to Lulu's first public demonstration in Cedartown actually began during a thunderstorm about two weeks before she made her initial stage appearance. She and her cousin Lora had gone to bed but were unable to sleep because they were frightened by the severe electrical storm. Then they heard what they described as muffled popping sounds. A search of the room failed to disclose the origin of the noise. When they went back to bed, the popping began again, this time apparently from beneath their pillows.

Lulu's parents were called and apprised of this state of affairs but they, too, failed to find any explanation or source. After watching and listening and searching for several hours, the rest of the family assured the two girls that it must be some phenomenon resulting from the severe electrical storm.

It was a convenient suggestion that lost its meaning the following night when Lulu's bed resounded with heavy thumps and sharp raps that could be plainly felt by the awe-stricken family when they placed their hands on the bedstead. Deacon Hurst called in some neighbors, more than a dozen in all, and they, too, were mystified and somewhat alarmed by the heavy pounding sounds that shook the walls of Lulu's bedroom. Someone inquired whether the sounds were coming from overhead and got what appeared to be a reply in the form of a prompt and resounding blow on the ceiling. Those present found that they could ask questions and get answers by simply requesting one knock for "yes" and two raps for "no."

This type of phenomenon is generally identified with what is called "poltergeist" activity and is almost always associated with children or, at least, adolescents. So it was in this case, for the activity was clearly identified with the presence of Lulu, who was then fourteen years old.

The really violent manifestations began on the fourth day after the pillow poppings, when Lulu picked up a chair to hand it to a visiting relative. The relative was flung against the wall so hard that she fell to the floor. Others grabbed the gyrating chair and got the same treatment. Even with four men hanging on to it, the force behind the chair was too much for them; it simply twisted the chair to pieces, leaving the men exhausted and alarmed. Lulu was in tears and ran screaming from the house.

These were the feats she reproduced countless times on the stage in the ensuing two years. Her second public presentation was at De Give's Opera House in Atlanta, which was jammed to the rafters with the curious.

There, in addition to the feats shown to the Cedartown audience, Lulu added two others. In one of them she simply touched the extended first two fingers of her right hand to the shaft of an ordinary billiard cue and two strong men who tried to force the cue tip to the floor exhausted themselves in failure.

Also for the wildly cheering Atlanta audience, she capped the climax by having three grown men sit on an ordinary kitchen chair, one atop the other. Lulu merely placed the open palms of her hands on the upright posts of the chair back, raised her hands slowly, and the chair with its three men aboard rose to a height of six inches above the stage and remained there for two minutes while a group of skeptical professors measured . . . and marveled.

When Lulu Hurst appeared before the faculty and students of the Medical College at Charleston, South Carolina, the physical arrangements were such that everything that transpired on the stage would be in full view of those who would be looking for trickery, an element that must have been well represented that evening.

Of this performance, the *Charleston News And Courier* had this to say:

". . . a more notable and critical audience could hardly be found. And we doubt if a more able and scientific body of men ever assembled in the State. . . . There was not a man in this distinguished and learned array who could explain the mysterious phenomenon. . . . Such was the interest awakened in the matter that Hibernian Hall was filled last night by the largest and most skeptical audience that has ever assembled in Charleston. Every seat was taken and the closest attention was paid to the performances on the stage, on which there poured a perfect flood of light. There was no chance for any deception, as the stage was open to the audience in front and the rear and sides of the stage were occupied by gentlemen, all of whom were eager to catch the slightest evidence of foul play."

Lulu's smashing success before the learned men of Charleston was typical of many such experiences. She gave

a private showing for the State Medical College in Augusta
and members of the faculty placed their hands between
hers and the objects. They felt no muscular tension yet the
strong men were thrown about violently, as always.

The uproar that preceded each appearance of this most
remarkable young lady was surpassed only by that which
ensued after she had given her exhibition. Thus, when her
parents made arrangements for Lulu to appear in Washington, D.C., there was an immediate demand that she subject
herself to the scrutiny of some of the nation's most eminent
scientists, a condition to which she readily agreed.

This special performance took place in the laboratory
of Professor Alexander Graham Bell and was attended by
twenty scientists whom he had invited from the Smithsonian
and the Naval Observatory staffs.

Was Lulu's power some form of electricity?

They placed her on a glass platform insulated by glass
rods and the 'power' demonstrated itself in full force.

Next they placed her on a platform connected with a
pair of scales. A 200 pound man sat down in a plain chair
which was off the scales. Lulu leaned forward, lifted man
and chair off the floor and held them there, but the scales
which should then have registered the combined weight of
Miss Hurst and the man she was lifting, registered his
weight alone! The startled scientists suspected that the scales
had gone awry and they checked at once. The scales
registered correctly when either or both parties involved
stood on them, but when Lulu picked up man and chair
her weight seemed to be nothing at all . . . or his weight
shrank to only a fraction of what it was.

The scientists checked her blood, measured her height
and weight, questioned her at length about this astounding

ability of hers. Lulu professed to know nothing of what it was or where it came from and certainly the scientists could offer no suggestions, for their own experiments had left them more puzzled than before.

Booked into Wallack's theatre in New York City by Charles Frohman, Lulu amazed and delighted her big city audiences by defeating the brawniest members of the New York Athletic Club. She played to five weeks of packed houses while the New York newspapers sang her praises.

After the triumph in New York came a swing around the country that took her to Boston, where she suffered stage fright and gave a mediocre performance, then on to Chicago, Cincinnati, Milwaukee and finally to Knoxville. By this time she had worked out an excellent finale for the show. After having thrown grown men about the stage like toys, she offered to give them a chance to return the treatment. Lulu held a billiard cue across her chest, stood on one foot and invited the men to shove her off balance. Not one of them ever succeeded.

It was in 1885, slightly more than two years after this amazing hegira began, that it all ended when Lulu Hurst told reporters that she was canceling all further exhibitions and returning to her home town to live the simple life with the young man she had married on the tour. Offers from Europe and Asia went unanswered—Lulu Hurst had had enough.

The reasons behind her dramatic exit from the performances that had made her rich in two fabulous years are subject to as many interpretations as the power that enabled her to accomplish her feats on the stage.

For some time after she made her dramatic and unexpected cessation of public appearances Lulu refused to comment on the 'act' itself. But she had left too many questions unanswered, too many scientists puzzled. Finally she 'explained'—but the explanation unquestionably failed to tell the entire story.

She said, "I had become burdened with the idea of the vast amount of superstition and delusion in the public mind concerning the 'Power.' . . . As my fame grew, the superstition of the people grew, and the burden grew likewise. While I knew the 'Power' was wonderful and apparently inexplicable, yet I did not like to be looked upon as some abnormal, quasi-supernatural sort of a being.

"I despised any sort of distinguished, famous, supernormal isolation from other people. . . . I knew the Spiritualists everywhere were pointing to me as the mighty 'Medium,' though I always disclaimed such an appellation. While I could not then explain the nature of such a 'Force' I always denounced such theories. My phenomenon was beginning to be used to prop up all sorts of outlandish and superstitious ideas and notions. This knowledge had oppressed me for a long time."

This was such palpable hokum that it failed utterly. It was unmistakably a statement that had been written for her by someone who did not know her intimately and who therefore did not know her educational limitations. Since neither of her parents was well educated either, the statement had been prepared by someone and handed to the girl for release. The demand for a real explanation continued.

Her next 'explanation' gave the subject still another twist. The original popping sounds, she asserted, were made by forcing a hatpin through the feather pillow as a childish prank. The raps were produced by pushing on the footboards with her toes; and the violence that twisted chairs apart and threw strong men about the stage were nothing more than what she called 'deflected force.' Pressed for a clarification on this rather vague point, Lulu could only describe it as "unrecognized mechanical principles involving leverage and balance" which, she claimed, caused force used against her to glance off and sometimes to "recoil on the user."

The records of the feats this 115 pound girl performed are abundant and well-attested. It is quite improbable that anyone, at this late date, will be able to discover the real answer to her remarkable abilities. It is also quite apparent that Lulu Hurst was not being perfectly candid with the reporters and scientists who sought the answers.

During the original period of poppings and rappings in her parents' home, the noises were noted at times when Lulu was NOT in the bed to play her 'childish pranks' with hatpins and pressure on the footboards. Some of the rappings were described by witnesses as resembling the pounding of a sledge hammer, which seems to rule out Lulu's belated explanation.

Time after time, during her tour, she underwent investigation and questioning by prominent scientists. And time after time she is on record as having told them that she did not know the source or workings of the 'power.' If she was telling the truth then, she certainly was not telling the truth two years later when she dismissed the whole thing as nothing but unknown principles of leverage that caused force used against her to rebound or to glance off.

The possibility that she resorted to optical illusion must be ruled out because of the test conditions under which she repeated everything she did on the stage. The use of stooges must also be ruled out, for the simple reason that among her opponents were respected athletes like those from the New York Athletic Club, and it would have been impossible to have kept such a secret with so many persons involved.

The solution to the riddle of Lulu Hurst seems to lie in the religious affiliations of her father, a Baptist deacon, and her uncle, a minister in a church near her home.

Like the churches they represented, both of these men were opposed to the public exploitation of the unknown forces which were manifested through this girl. The more exhibitions she gave, the more people were affected by what they saw, and which science could not explain. All in all, it added up to a tremendous boost for Spiritualism and organized religion quickly recognized the threat.

After Lulu had been on the tour about a year a new factor entered into her existence. At every city where she appeared she and her parents were met by groups of ministers who made it plain that her 'power' was a matter of grave concern and that they would pray for her to be relieved of this 'burden.' It was a well-organized pressure play which neither Lulu nor her parents seemed to recognize as such.

After Lulu's parents left the tour she was managed by the young man whom she later married. Money was rolling in, not only from the public performances but also from the percentage she received for the use of her magic name on soap, soft drinks, cigars and even on plows, which were advertised as "Strong as Lulu Hurst!"

With all the money she would ever need; with the young man she wanted for a husband; with constant pressure on her parents to get her off the stage, Lulu waited until she was once again near her home and then walked out of the limelight.

Her first 'explanation' was plainly a prefabricated piece of twaddle that was beyond her academic capacities, aimed at ridiculing Spiritualism. Her second 'explanation' if true, meant that she had repeatedly lied to the scientists throughout the entire two years of her tour and that her parents had joined in the deception. This, too, may be dismissed as highly improbable.

This leaves us with the record of her incredible feats, and of consistent scientific failures to identify them as applications of natural law. Since scientists could not explain them because they did not understand them, it would be uncharitable of us if we failed to excuse fifteen-year-old Lulu Hurst on the same grounds.

9

The Woman Who Came Back From The Dead

For some reason which she did not divulge, Mrs. Theresa Butler took an overdose of sleeping tablets at her home in San Francisco on November 8, 1952. She was found in the bathtub hours later and, after the coroner determined that she had no blood pressure, no perceptible reflexes and neither heartbeat nor breathing, he pronounced her dead and sent the body to the morgue.

An attendant got the surprise of his life when he saw the "corpse" working its jaw and gasping. The lady got another ride—this time to the hospital. There she lay in a coma for five days. On the evening of the fifth day after her "death" she was able to recognize her daughter and Dr. J. C. Geiger, the city-county public health director.

A few days later she was returned to her home and the medics went back to ponder the question of when is a person dead—and how can a doctor tell?

Said Dr. Geiger: "By the accepted tests Mrs. Butler had died from that overdose of sleeping tablets. There were no detectable signs of life whatever. She was clinically dead.

Yet she is now alive and well. Apparently we are going to have to revise our opinions of what constitutes the irrefutable criteria of death."

Dr. Thomas Albers, Superintendent of the San Francisco Hospital told colleagues and newsmen: "This is the most far-fetched and implausible case I have ever known. She was dead. She could not recover. It just couldn't happen, but it did."

The numerous physicians who examined her predicted that she would recover fully and planned to study her progress from time to time to see what might be the after effects, if any, of her return from "death."

10

The Lost Colony

One of the most fascinating mysteries of early American history is the unsolved disappearance of Sir Walter Raleigh's colony which vanished from Roanoke Island, North Carolina. The fate that befell those hapless pioneers was never officially determined, even though the answer may have been crying for attention all the while.

When they were last seen by their own countrymen, there were one hundred and seventeen men, women and children living in the tiny settlement on Roanoke Island. They had pleaded to be taken away. They were surrounded by hostile Indians and they professed to be short on food, which was probably true. As the vessel on which they sought succor dropped over the horizon, a curtain fell over the unhappy settlers, a curtain which held its secret for at least a century.

When Sir Walter Raleigh's supply ship finally arrived at Roanoke, it found the village deserted. There were no traces of massacre and no signs of battle. Neither were there any notes which might have been left to guide a rescue party. Just a post on which one word had been carved—the word "Croatan."

It is possible that the word meant little or nothing to the Englishmen who found it. Or if they did recognize it as a clue to the missing colonists, perhaps they realized that they dared not follow the clue to its conclusion. At any rate, they made no effort to do anything about it. The colony was written off as lost without a trace, and so it remained for a hundred years.

The first hint of the possible fate of the Roanoke colony came in 1719 when venturesome white hunters entered the area now known as Robeson County, North Carolina, about two hundred miles inland from Roanoke. There, in the villages of the Croatan Indians, they found a most unusual race of people. They were lighter skinned than the surrounding tribes, and lived in well planned villages. Furthermore, these unusual "Indians" spoke English with many of the idioms that had been in use at the time the colonists disappeared. And they tilled the soil with slaves, mostly Indian captives. The white hunters talked with them, puzzled over the strange mixture of languages and customs, and went away.

The census of Robeson County for 1790 also furnishes some interesting material for speculation and study.

For instance, among the missing colonists there were ninety-five family names. The first census of Robeson County Indians shows that fifty-four of these same family names were to be found there. But the same names were found nowhere else, even among the whites, in such concentration at the time.

Also of interest to researchers is the fact that many of the missing colonists had come from Scoville Town, in England. The Croatan village which was replete with English family names similar to those of the missing

Roanoke pioneers was called Scuffletown, the common colloquialism for Scoville Town.

At the time the white hunters first noted the unusual nature of the Croatans, the Indians told of their blue-eyed ancestors who "talked in books." There was also the evidence of the well planned villages, the advanced methods of farming, the language studded with English phrases and idioms, the advanced states of the Croatans' arts and crafts.

Precisely what happened to the missing colonists may never be known. Yet they managed to carve on a post the word "Croatan"—an Indian nation that used slaves. That clue on the post, and the additional evidence found long afterward among the Croatans themselves, may indeed provide the answer to the riddle of Roanoke.

Captured, carried away and forced to spend their lives among the Croatans, they managed to leave clues to their fate in the customs and culture of their captors which exist even to this day.

That one word "Croatan" was almost certainly a cry for help that never came.

11

The Mystery of Molly Fancher

Precisely what happened to Molly Fancher was never clearly defined, although this omission was not due to lack of investigation and experimentation.

According to the medical records kept by the family physician, Dr. Samuel F. Spier, of Brooklyn, Molly was a very normal, healthy girl until that February 3, 1866 when she complained of feeling dizzy and a moment later slumped to the floor in the kitchen of her mother's home at 60 Steven Court.

The mother thought she had fainted and gave her a routine treatment but, when Molly failed to regain consciousness after half an hour, Dr. Spier was summoned. He reported that he found her in a trance-like state and that he could not diagnose the condition on such short notice. The physician expressed the belief that the girl would be all right by morning.

Molly was not all right by morning. The days dragged into weeks, and months—but Molly Fancher remained in the death-like coma that had taken possession of her without warning.

Dr. Spier noted that her breathing had become almost indistinguishable; her pulse was so faint that there were times when it seemed non-existent; her body was as clammy as that of a corpse. The bewildered physician took counsel with his fellow medics and they too could offer no assistance, for none of them had ever dealt with such a case. They came, they saw, they examined and they shook their heads.

Nine years later Molly Fancher was still lying there insensible, somewhere between life and death. The record shows that during that time she had eaten virtually nothing; in Dr. Spier's words, "about the amount a normal person would consume in two days!"

By this time her case had become a cause célèbre throughout the medical profession, and rightly so, for it constituted a challenge they could scarcely ignore. But there were other surprises waiting for them one afternoon in 1875 when Dr. Spier asked several of his colleagues to come to a meeting at his office.

"Gentlemen," he said, "none of us has ever dealt with a case like this before. The physical condition of this young lady is baffling enough—but now I find that she is endowed with some sort of supernatural power!"

Among those present at the meeting was the noted neurologist, Dr. Robert Ormiston, of Boston. He was openly skeptical and there was more than a hint of this in his voice when he said: "Just what is this so-called supernatural power of Miss Fancher?"

Spier was ready for them. He invited them to meet with him a few days later at the bedside of the unconscious girl, to witness for themselves the things that he had categorized as "supernatural." In addition to Dr. Ormiston, Dr. Spier invited the famed astronomer, Dr. Richard Parkhurst, and another noted physician, Dr. Willard Parker, New York neurologist.

After they had discussed the case at length and studied the charts Dr. Spier had kept, they noted the unnaturally weak pulse and breathing and the subnormal temperature.

Then Dr. Spier said: "Gentlemen, this girl can fully describe the dress and actions of persons hundreds of miles from here, just as they are this instant! Furthermore, she can read unopened letters and books!"

Dr. Willard and Dr. Parker left the room and held a whispered conference outside the house. They agreed that a letter was to be placed inside three sealed envelopes in Dr. Spier's office, about five miles away from where they then stood. They would ask the girl if she could tell them what was in the letter and, after her reply had been taken down and attested by all those present, they would compare it with the contents of their own sealed envelope.

While their messenger was en route to Dr. Spier's office, they returned to the girl's bedside. Dr. Parkhurst asked her if she could tell them what was in the envelopes. She hesitated a moment and then whispered: "It is a letter—in three sealed envelopes in Dr. Spier's office. Written on a sheet of paper are the words, 'Lincoln was shot by a crazed actor.' "

Spier, Parkhurst, Willard and Ormistan all went to Spier's office and there they opened the letter. It contained the exact message the unconscious girl had stated.

The man who had taken the sealed message from the Fancher home to Dr. Spier's office, Peter Graham of 23 West 60th Street, New York City, was beyond suspicion. He was a personal friend of Dr. Willard and had made the trip with him that day.

For still another test the same day, the doctors decided to ask Miss Fancher to describe the appearance and activities of a distant person, as Dr. Spier had asserted she could do.

They went back to the Fancher home and asked the girl if she could describe to them the appearance and where-abouts of Peter Graham's brother, Frank, who was then somewhere in New York City.

Without hesitation Miss Fancher replied, giving his detailed description, even to mentioning a missing button from the right sleeve of his coat. She also told the puzzled gentlemen present that Frank Graham had left work earlier than customary because he had a splitting headache.

A check by telegraph confirmed everything that the girl had said, even to the headache.

Molly Fancher lay in that trance-like condition for forty-six years. Her parents and Dr. Spier had long since died when she finally regained consciousness in 1912, a medical case that had attracted world wide attention.

Her ailment, like her strange talent, was never ex-plained. Molly Fancher passed away quietly in her sleep at the age of seventy-three in March of 1915.

12

Idiot Geniuses

You have often heard it said that the line of distinction between genius and idiocy is a very thin one. I propose to show you that sometimes the line is nonexistent; that the two extremes can exist in the same mind.

Before us we have the picture of a pitiable creature who spent practically all of his life in the insane asylum at Armentieres, France. Dr. A. F. Tredgold reports the case of M. Fleury in his monumental work, *Mental Deficiency*.

Fleury was the child of syphilitic parents. He was born blind and feeble-minded. Abandoned at a very early age, he became an inmate of the institution, where it was soon noticed that he had a marked flair for mental arithmetic. Attempts to teach him the common decencies were fruitless; Fleury could grasp little of what was explained to him. Stooped, shuffling of gait, bleary-eyed and harmless, he spent his life fumbling his way around the halls and grounds of the institution which was the only home he ever had.

But there were times when Fleury stepped out of his cocoon of idiocy to astound the scientists. Those were the occasions when learned men assembled to test his alleged ability as a lightning calculator; times when they invariably went away wiser but much more baffled, for Fleury could perform feats of calculation with a speed and accuracy that defied explanation.

Once, before a group of twelve of Europe's top scholars and mathematicians, Fleury was brought into the room for an exhibition of his incredible talents. He leaned against the wall, simpering, embarrassed at being in the presence of strangers. His attendant read to him the question which the learned men had propounded: If you have sixty-four boxes and you place one grain of corn in the first box, and twice as much in each succeeding box as the box it follows, how many grains of corn must you place in the sixty-fourth box?

Fleury continued to giggle and hide his face from the professors. His attendant asked if he understood the question. Yes, he did. Did he know the answer? Yes, he did. In less than half a minute he had calculated the correct figure: 18,446,734,073,709,551,615.

Fleury, the idiot of Armentieres, was called upon to perform similar feats for astronomers, architects, bankers, tax collectors and ship builders. Each time he produced the correct answer in a matter of seconds, a performance which could not be duplicated until the advent of electronic calculators, decades after his death.

Similar in some ways to the case of Fleury is that of Tom Wiggins, an imbecile born to a slave girl who worked in the manor house of a family named Bethune, in 1849, in Alabama. Tom was also blind, and because he needed so much care he was permitted to live in the big house with his mother. He developed the ability to grope his way around the house without assistance, but preferred to stand motionless for hours in the corner under the big main stairway, evidently fascinated by the ticking of the grandfather's clock.

One delightful spring evening in 1855, when Tom was six years old, the Bethunes entertained some visitors from Montgomery and among the entertainments were two piano recitations by the Bethune ladies, one of them the owner of the plantation and the other her daughter-in-law. Both were accomplished musicians who had studied at Boston conservatories.

After the guests had retired for the night, the younger Mrs. Bethune was surprised to hear piano music. Had her mother-in-law gone back downstairs at that unusual hour to resume her playing? A quick check showed that the lady was sleeping soundly. Puzzled, Mrs. Bethune tiptoed back down stairs and to the door of the room where the piano was located.

By the moonlight streaming in from the tall windows she saw little blind Tom seated at the instrument, his stubby fingers feeling their way across the keyboard. Haltingly, but unmistakably, he was duplicating one of the melodies that had been played by the ladies earlier in the evening. After groping his way through it once, as though to familiarize himself with it, he suddenly started anew and duplicated both tempo and music, exactly as he had heard it a few hours before.

The child had crawled through an open window into the drawing room—to the keyboard of a piano which he had never before so much as touched, and was repeating note for note the music that had been performed by trained pianists.

Tom Wiggins, the blind imbecile, became Blind Tom the musical prodigy. The Bethunes discovered that his remarkable gift was that of faultless imitation. Any number that they played he could instantly repeat, exactly as they had played it, including any mistakes they might have made.

The word of his amazing talent spread rapidly and Mrs. Bethune permitted him to be exhibited, first in the major Southern cities and later in New York, Chicago, Cincinnati and other cities around the nation.

Blind Tom spent about twenty-five years touring this country and Europe, winning acclaim wherever he appeared for his ability to listen to a great pianist and then to duplicate his performance faithfully and instantly, even to the most subtle shades of expression. The money that poured in from these tours was managed by the younger Mrs. Bethune, who prudently established a fund which enabled Tom to live in comfort throughout his life.

How blind Tom Wiggins, the imbecile pianist, ever acquired knowledge of the keyboard was an unsolved mystery. As a child he did not have access to the room where the piano was kept and he was unable to tell the Bethunes if he had ever tried to play before the night of Mrs. Bethune's discovery.

As a traveling pianist and a mature man of two hundred and fifty pounds, with the mind of a baby, he presented many problems. Ofttimes he would throw his food about like a petulant child, and many times, when an audience had applauded him at one of his performances, Blind Tom would show his delight by standing on his head in the middle of the stage, a feat that is not looked upon with favor on the concert platform.

Blind Tom Wiggins, the idiot concert pianist, gradually

lost his incredible talents. By middle age he had again re-
verted to a drooling, helpless imbecile, and as such he died
in 1907, supported by the proceeds from his fantastic
career.

To a wealthy family in Berne, Switzerland, in 1768,
was born a son christened Gottfried Mind. The signs of
mental deficiency which he showed as a baby soon developed into the unmistakable indications of imbecility. Being
wealthy, the family made every effort to develop the child's
intelligence, but he failed to respond. From his birth to
the time of his death at the age of forty-six in 1814,
Gottfried Mind was a moron, unable to care for himself;
a creature who had to be accompanied by a bodyguard
when he went for walks.

Gottfried received a set of paints, some chalk and slates,
when he was a child. Shortly thereafter he began to amuse
himself by drawing remarkably lifelike sketches of animals
and children, and some of them he rendered in water colors.
On sunny days his guard would lead poor Gottfried to
various quiet nooks on the family estate and for hours he
would sit there, mumbling to himself happily, drawing or
painting whatever pleased his childlike mind.

By the time he was thirty years old this pitiful fellow
had become noted throughout Europe for the quality of
his work as an artist. He was especially renowned for
pictures of pets, which he loved, and of children, with
whom he was mentally akin. A picture of a cat with kittens,
painted by Gottfried Mind, was purchased by King
George IV of England and hung for many years in the
palace.

This strange mixture of artist and idiot has a modern counterpart in the person of Kyoshi Yamashita of Kobe, Japan. Like Gottfried Mind, he must be protected and led about like a child, yet his paintings have won such wide acclaim that in late 1957, when they were to be shown in a Kobe department store, the crowd that turned out to see and buy was estimated at more than one hundred thousand persons.

Born in the slums of Tokyo, Kyoshi was so retarded mentally that he had to be placed in an institution at the age of twelve. Although he had no family background in art and although he had not shown any previous interest in it himself, Kyoshi began making pictures by tearing up colored paper and sticking the bits together on canvas.

His talents continued to develop. Doctors at the institution encouraged him by giving him paints, which at first he ate like candy, then stubby brushes with which he soon learned to paint. Today he is a national favorite in Japan. Magazines vie for his work for cover illustrations. One of the best selling books in Japan in 1956 was a volume of color prints by thirty-four-year-old Kyoshi Yamashita, who was then roaming through the streets of the city, begging, unaware of his own whereabouts.

Because he is unable to care for himself, ofttimes wandering out into the streets naked, this talented imbecile is under the care of a government-appointed guardian. But occasionally he slips away and roams the streets, dirty, ragged, living off what he can beg until authorities find him again.

Dr. Ryuzaburo Shikiba, one of Japan's top psychiatrists, says of Kyoshi Yamashita: "An idiot-savant—a riddle and a challenge to science."

Further emphasizing the ephemeral line between idiocy and genius is the case of Jeffrey Janet, who was born in Ilford, England, in 1945—born spastic, crippled and blind. Doctors examined the twisted little boy and told the parents, "He will be an imbecile; he can't live more than a couple of years at most."

Jeffrey Janet not only lived but he became a most remarkable lad whose talents constitute sheer genius. By the time he was 16 years old, still blind and so badly crippled that walking was impossible for him, Jeffrey was demonstrating some astounding capabilities.

Doctors and newsmen were present at a demonstration where Jeffrey recited, without error and in rapid fire sequence, every one of the hundreds of programs on British radio and television for an entire week. He did this after they had been read to him only once.

This "imbecile who couldn't live two years" also performed complex mathematical problems for his audience, snapping the answers almost as soon as he had been given the problems. And by some method which he has devised for himself, Jeffrey Janet can work out in a few seconds the day of the week on which any day will fall in the future, or on which it fell in the past, even allowing for the changes in the calendar.

His fantastic development in defiance of medical experience merely underscores how little we really know about the wonderland of the human mind.

13

The Predictions Of
The Uncanny
Robert Nixon

The dirty, ragged, bare-legged boy dropped the reins on the plow handles and acted like one gone berserk. He jumped up and down, ran a few steps across the fresh furrows and shouted at the top of his voice. Other plowmen in adjoining fields went on about their work; to them it was just another antic by that idiotic son of the illiterate Nixon family.

But this time it was much more than that, for Robert Nixon was that rarity who combined idiocy, which is little understood, with clairvoyance, which is even less understood.

The overseer of Bridge House Farm, in Cheshire, England, noted the antics of young Nixon and when they persisted, went to get the boy back on the job. But when he drew near enough to make out what the feeble-minded plowboy was saying the overseer stopped to listen.

There had been rumors that two great armies were massing for a battle—but that was at Bosworth Field—a long distance from Cheshire. The overseer remembered that Robert Nixon had been saying for weeks that King Richard would fight with Henry, the Earl of Richmond, at Bosworth. Now the boy was frantic with excitement—eyes glazed—waving his arms wildly. It was well that the overseer kept his distance for Nixon was flailing about himself with the long whip he carried, punctuating his frenzied screams by cracking the whip like pistol shots.

"Now, Richard!" Nixon shouted. "Now! — There — Now!"

He paused and stood transfixed, staring off into the distance.

"Up, Henry! Up with all arms!—Over the ditch Henry! Over the ditch and the battle is won!"

By this time some of the other workers had gathered silently behind the overseer to observe this strange tableau of the bewitched plowboy. They saw him stand silent and glassy-eyed, drooling, his mouth twitching.

Then a smile crept over the boy's face.

For the first time he became aware of the presence of his awe-stricken audience. "The battle is over," said young Nixon, "and Henry has won!"

With that he picked up the reins and went back to his work as though nothing unusual had happened.

The overseer ordered the other plowmen back to their tasks before he hurried away to make his report to his masters, the Lords of Cholmondeley. They had heard that this unfortunate lad had some way of knowing things that transpired at a distance as well as things that were going to happen at some later date.

Robert Nixon had correctly predicted the death of a member of the Cholmondeley family. He had foretold a great storm two weeks in advance and had declared that Richard and Henry would fight at Bosworth Field. Now he was claiming that they had fought . . . and that Richard had been defeated and driven from the throne. Time would tell.

Two days later messengers from the new King arrived at the little village to break the tidings to the taxpayers, only to discover that the people there already knew of Henry's ascension to the throne. But how could they? Through Robert Nixon, the idiot plowboy who could see things far beyond the horizon and sometimes into the future. The messengers rode away to break the news to other, less fortunate, villages.

About two weeks after the King's messengers had left the village, Robert Nixon ran from door to door, pleading for some place to hide. The King's men were coming to take him to the palace, he screamed, and if he went to the Palace he would starve to death!

In spite of his tearful pleadings, nobody would hide him. It was just too ridiculous to consider, this idea that the King would send for the village idiot. Nixon was hooted and jeered from the streets.

Yet, he had been correct in his anticipation of being called to the Palace. He was working in the kitchen when he turned to his mother and said: "I must go now. The King's men are not far away. I will never come back!"

The messengers found this strange boy ready when they arrived. King Henry was also ready when Robert Nixon got to the Palace, for the King was skeptical of the reports he had been given about the remarkable talents of the boy. To test him, King Henry had concealed a ring and when Nixon was brought into his presence the King told him that he had lost the ring and that he expected the boy to tell him where it was.

Without hesitation Nixon replied: "He who hideth can find."

The King laughed with the rest of his court, and ordered that a scribe be assigned to Nixon's presence at all times, in order that any predictions that might be made should be recorded and brought to court.

Many of Nixon's predictions have survived, thanks to the King's orders in the fifteenth century. His story was investigated by Lady Cowper in 1670 and again by the Bishop of Ely. As late as 1845 new material was added to the documentation when still another manuscript of Nixon's prophecies was unearthed among the heirlooms of his family. He made hundreds of predictions, most of them short range projections of little historical significance. But almost all of them were fulfilled by events and individuals, as he specified. Still unfulfilled are two grim prophecies as follows:

"Foreign nations shall invade England with snow on their helms. . . . The bear that had been long tied to a stake shall shake off his chains and cause much debate."

And again, he said: "For though the world be at peace —and with peace at night the nations ring—men shall rise to war in the morning."

Robert Nixon, the feeble-minded plowboy from the tiny village of Over, became a favorite of King Henry. He was given the run of the castle and seldom wanted for anything. All went well until the King planned a lengthy hunting trip which did not include provisions for Nixon to accompany him. As soon as the boy heard of this he ran to the King and pleaded to be allowed to go along—or at least to be allowed to return home and stay with his parents in the King's absence.

The King asked why Nixon was so eager to leave the palace and when the boy told him that he was afraid of starving to death in the King's absence, the monarch broke into roars of laughter. To allay Nixon's fears Henry appointed a special deputy to be personally responsible for the boy's well-being while the King was away.

The deputy took the job seriously. When some of the servants teased the poor feeble-minded lad the deputy locked Nixon in a room to which only the deputy had the key, and he warned all others to refrain from entering that room. When the deputy was called away on the King's business he forgot to assign anyone to take care of Nixon, locked in a room to which only the deputy had access. When the King returned two weeks later he found Nixon dead, from lack of food and water.

Robert Nixon's most absurd prophecy had been fulfilled. He had died of starvation in the King's palace.

14

People Who Saw Without Eyes

The first white men to visit the Samoan Islands were understandably skeptical when the natives insisted that some of their blind persons could see through their skin. Could they prove it? The natives brought several of the blind before the whites and the blind described the visitors in detail.

Just another trick of the treacherous natives, said the all-knowing whites, who then proceeded with their original plan of rape and pillage, things they really understood. The demonstrations were written up in the log books and in the reports for the King, and then forgotten.

Even to this day it is not clear just what did happen there but there is some evidence to support the claims of the Samoans.

In France, shortly after the end of the first World War, Dr. Jules Romain undertook experiments to determine what truth, if any, existed in the rumors that some persons could see without the use of their eyes. He found the results so intriguing that he continued the tests on both blind and sighted persons for many years.

Dr. Romain found that the ability varied from one individual to another and that it also varied with the mental and physical condition of the subjects. It was particularly frustrating to find that a person who performed brilliantly one day might fail miserably the next day, especially if something had happened to put that subject emotionally or physically below par.

But Romain continued his experiments, sometimes in the presence of such noted (and extremely critical) witnesses as Anatole France, who admitted that he had gone to sneer and had come away astounded.

Dr. Romain was of the opinion that sight without eyes might be possible because of certain microscopic nerve ends in the skin, the little-understood Ranvier's manisci. These nerve ends, reasoned Romain, might have evolved through the ages into the more complex form known as eyes.

By patiently testing hundreds of subjects, he found a few who could distinguish between light and dark—but when he interposed a metal shield between the skin of the cheeks and the light, these same persons could not detect the difference between light and dark. Further tests indicated that some persons were photosensitive in small areas of skin, including several subjects who were most sensitive on their noses and three cases who possessed photosensitivity to an acute degree in their finger tips.

His work ended in 1924, and fellow scientists dismissed his reports and findings as "unscientific" and "incomplete" —and adopted a policy of wait and see.

The lengthy experiments of Dr. Romain were by no means the first instances where an eminent medic took cognizance of this ability to "see through the skin." Dr.

Cesare Lombroso, noted neurologist and psychiatrist, had such an outstanding reputation that his name alone squelched possible detractors. And Dr. Lombroso stated his experience for the world to see in his book *After Death— What?*

He reported that a fourteen-year-old girl who had been quite normal in every respect suddenly developed symptoms of hysteria. She failed to respond to medical treatment and her condition steadily worsened, from dyspepsia and vomiting to inability to eat solid food, severe loss of weight and convulsions. Three months after the attack began she was totally blind.

Then she developed the surprising ability to see, even though it was quite evident that her eyes were not functioning at all. Dr. Lombroso and the family physician conducted tests which showed that the girl was "seeing" with the tip of her nose and the lobe of her left ear!

To eliminate the possibility that the eyes were somehow involved, the doctors placed thick blindfolds over the patient's eyes and held the test material at an angle which nullified the chance of any peeping. Still the child passed the tests without difficulty.

Lombroso says that she read a letter while blindfolded and that she was able to identify colors without error. When a bright light was shone against the ear lobe she winced; when he poked his finger at the tip of her nose she jumped back and angrily inquired: "Are you trying to blind me?"

The remarkable transposition of senses was not limited to sight alone in this case, for Dr. Lombroso reports that her sense of smell had also undergone a change of location. When strong amonia was held under her nose she gave no reaction; but when it was held under her chin she cried out in pain. By this same means she could distinguish the fragrance of flowers.

Confronted with such a bewildering display of the unconventional, it is small wonder that Dr. Lombroso showed little surprise when the same young girl's sense of smell eventually moved to her foot.

Perhaps Dr. Lombroso knew that there were medical precedents for such cases. In *Electricite Animale,* Lyons, 1808, a Dr. Petetin reported the cases of eight women whose senses had become localized in the finger tips and the solar plexus region.

In 1840, in the publication *Giornale dell Academicia di Medicina,* an Italian physician reported at length on the strange case of a fourteen-year-old farm girl whose fits of hysteria included periods of somnambulism during which she could see quite distinctly with the palms of her hands, to such an extent that she could distinguish colors and match ribbons.

At the University of Torino, 1821, there is in *Prazeos Medicae* a report on a Mr. Baerkmann who suffered a head injury in a fall and subsequently found that his sense of hearing had transferred to his solar plexus. The report says that this anomaly "was a matter of considerable wonder"— for which we can pardon the medics; for it would be a subject of considerable wonder in our own day.

The Rector of St. Phillip's Cathedral in Atlanta, Dean Raimundo de Ovies, reported shortly before World War II the case of a member of the parish who could be completely blindfolded but who could then identify objects held behind his back by placing the palms of his hands over them.

A very recent case of sight under prohibitive circumstances was one which would have been most heartening to the late Dr. Jules Romain.

When fifteen-year-old Margaret Foos walked into the room where the medical experts were waiting for her, she appeared to be just a normal, ordinary, healthy teenager. When she walked out of that same room two hours later, she left behind her twenty-five astonished and bewildered experts.

Margaret spent the first fourteen years of her life in the little Virginia community of Ellerson, where her father worked as foreman of a salvage warehouse for the Chesapeake and Ohio Railroad. Mr. Foos says that he noticed that the youngsters who played with his own would often indulge in blindfold games, and that some of the children showed more ability than others while blindfolded, at least more ability to avoid or locate large objects, such as trees. Margaret, said her father, showed this talent to a surprising degree and he first thought that she was seeing through or around the blindfold. When he took measures to prevent any peeping, she still manifested evidence of full sight and his interest in the matter was heightened. Some of the other youngsters seemed to possess the ability in varying degrees but none to the extent which Margaret finally attained.

He told a group of medical experts at the Veterans Administration Center, on a January afternoon in 1960, that it was his belief that Margaret's rapid progress was largely possible because she had complete trust in him and had confidence in his instructions. After blindfolding her, he would tell her that she was going to be able to see, impressing on her that she must believe this in order to accomplish it.

By the end of three weeks, said Mr. Foos, the child was able to point out large objects such as tables and doors, and shortly thereafter to locate and describe smaller objects: books, hats, clocks and wads of paper. This in turn led to her becoming able to describe color and texture of objects and even to reading print from newspapers.

This last talent was possible only after Margaret had failed repeatedly to bring the print into focus. Her father says he had no idea what to do to correct this so he just suggested to her that she should "blow" the smoke away, mentally, and to their surprise that solved the problem.

To say that the medical experts were skeptical at this point in the examination would probably be a gross understatement. Here was a railroader, with no medical training whatever, assuring them that he had trained this child to read and distinguish colors without the use of her eyes. It was preposterous! Preposterous to all except those who may have dimly recalled the work of Dr. Jules Romain thirty-five years previously.

Could Mr. Foos support his claims under test conditions—the conditions imposed by the doctors?

On that memorable afternoon the doctors blindfolded the young girl to their own satisfaction. This included not only the conventional wads of cotton and bandage but liberal applications of tape to make doubly sure that normal sight would not, and could not, be involved.

Under these conditions, fourteen-year-old Margaret Foos startled the experts by reading excerpts from the Bible, reading sections chosen at random from magazines and newspapers, identifying colors in various advertisements, playing checkers and identifying random objects selected by the doctors.

It was a dramatic and baffling demonstration of seeing where sight should have been impossible. Was it fraud? Was the child peeking under or through the bandages? The doctors had bandaged her themselves and in such a manner that, in their opinions, fraud was not possible. She had remained in their sight every second during the entire test and there was no chance of tampering. When the medics removed the tape and bandages, the heavy crisscross strips of the tape were centered over the front of the eyes, making an opaque patch through which she could not possibly have seen the test material without tilting her head back in order to bypass the tape.

Columnist Drew Pearson, reporting the test in his widely syndicated newspaper feature, says that one psychiatrist who was present for the tests said to him after the session was over: "It's conceivable that some new portion of the brain may have been discovered."

Margaret Foos was subsequently presented to the public on a network television show, the "People Are Funny" program, on both January 15 and 22, 1960.

From Scotland in 1956 came the report of a blind boy who was trained to "see" through his skin. The report was authorized by Dr. Karl Konig, superintendent of the Camphill Rudolph Steiner schools.

According to Dr. Konig, the school had received this blind lad when he was only four years old, a pitiable youngster who was considered uneducable, and who was able to talk only in harsh, rasping, parrot fashion.

As an experiment the child was placed on a couch and

surrounded by a screen of white sheets to exclude extraneous light. Then bright colored lights were played on him and on the sheets for varying periods of time.

Soon, says the doctor's report, the child was beginning to react to certain colors. He learned to speak properly and to sing and recite poems. He became sturdy and healthy and even the texture of his skin changed noticeably as his general condition improved. It was quite apparent to the medics that this child could distinguish lights of different colors and intensities by some means other than his sightless eyes.

Dr. Konig also reports on another interesting case at the same institution in which a blind and deaf child was placed in a darkened room and bathed in bright beams of colored light. Later a lighted candle was placed between pupil and teacher and soon the child was able to follow exactly the gestures made by the teacher. Dr. Konig reported that the child's eyes today have an expression of interest and personality. And most amazing, he "sees" small objects at distances up to six feet with sufficient clarity to enable him to pick them up from the floor, unassisted.

Another book in this particular field is *Face To Face* by Ved Mehta, published by Atlantic-Little, Brown in 1957. It tells the story of the author, a young Hindu, who became totally blind as the result of meningitis when he was only three years old. As a boy, Ved was able to ride his bicycle through the crowded streets of his home town in India. As a college student in the United States he was often at odds with officials who insisted that he carry the customary white cane of the blind, which Ved insisted he did not need or want. And it is known that he hitchhiked all over the United States without assistance.

How does he do it? Ved Mehta claims that he has what he calls "facial vision" by which he is able to make his way about, avoiding collisions and moving vehicles. He can't explain exactly how he does it—but he says he literally "sees" with his face, through the skin.

By whatever process, evidence from Dr. Romain to Dr. Konig and Ved Mehta indicates that sight without eyes can sometimes be developed.

15

The Baffling Brain

The brain, as every doctor knows, is the seat of our consciousness. It is of such delicate disposition that nature has protected it with a heavy helmet of bone. A sharp jar will cause the brain to lose its control of the owner's voluntary nervous system for varying periods of time, depending somewhat on the violence of the shock and the location or manner of delivery. This fact, known to the ancients, served as the basis for a crude form of anesthesia among the Egyptians. When they were ready to operate, they simply tapped the patient on top of the head with a leather-covered mallet until consciousness fled. This treatment could be, and *was*, repeated as needed.

In their monumental work *Anomalies and Curiosities of Medicine*, Drs. Gould and Pyle report several cases of severe brain damage which had little apparent effect on the victims.

They cite the case of a woman who worked (1879) in a mill. A huge bolt fell into the machinery and was thrown out with bullet-like force, striking the woman near the hairline above her right eye. The heavy bolt drove bits of bone ahead of it as it bored four inches into her skull.

A small amount of brain substance was lost at the time of the accident and a bit more when the doctors removed the bolt.

Although there was no reason to hope that she might recover, the girl not only regained consciousness but suffered no discomfort from her brain damage, not even a headache. Two years later when medics finally examined her and released her from treatment, her only memento of the incident was a small scar where the bolt had entered. She lived forty-two years after her accident.

She was more fortunate in some respects than the case reported by Job Van Meekren in his *Chirurgical Observations,* wherein he recounts the plight of a Russian nobleman who was dragged by a runaway horse. The poor fellow's head struck some stones and a part of his skull was torn away. Surgeons replaced the lost bone with a fragment from the skull of a newly-killed dog and the man recovered. Van Meekren says that although the nobleman regained perfect health, the clergy ordered him excommunicated and refused to reinstate him until he submitted to removal of the bit of dog bone from his skull.

One of the hazards of canal-boating is the danger of striking, or being struck by, some of the occasional bridges which have such restricted clearance that boatmen have to stoop—or pay the penalty.

The Medical Press of Western New York (1888) sets forth at length the case af a deck hand on a canal boat who was caught between a bridge timber and the super-structure of the boat. While he was thus held, as in a great vise, the sharp corner of the timber sheared off a portion of the hapless fellow's head. The excision began about two inches above his right eye and resulted in the loss of about one-fourth of the skull; in all, the aperture was about seven inches from front to back and about six inches wide.

Doctors who treated him a few hours after the accident found that the wound was as clean of soft parts as though it had been made with a surgeon's saw. There had been a substantial loss of brain matter and of blood.

For more than an hour the surgeons worked to close the gaping wound. Toward the end of that time, the victim opened his eyes and inquired what had happened. At the conclusion of the bandaging he sat up and, before the astonished doctors could prevent it, he got to his feet and began putting on his clothes, as though nothing had happened. Two months after the accident he was back at work on the canal boat and the case history shows that other than occasional dizzy spells he seemed to be in good health. Twenty-six years after the accident he had developed a pronounced unsteadiness in his walk and partial paralysis of the left leg and arm.

This remarkable fellow, with a concave area in his head extending from crown to ear, was back in the hospital in Buffalo in 1887, thirty years after the accident. He was subsequently released after the doctors there noted in their reports that he showed a marked tendency to hysteria, sobbing like a child when he was scolded.

Another interesting case is now in the Museum of the Massachusetts Medical College. It is the cast of a human skull with a heavy iron rod, three feet long and weighing thirteen pounds, driven through it.

This grisly memento is from one of the most famous of all accident cases involving the human brain—the so called American Crowbar Case.

On the afternoon of September 13, 1847, a twenty-five

year-old foreman on the Rutland and Burlington Railroad, Phineas Gage, was tamping some explosive into a hole, preparatory to blasting. He was kneeling over the hole, ramming the powder down with an iron bar about one and one-half inches in diameter, sharpened to a point on the upper end and ground off flat on the lower end. It seems not to have occurred to anyone that the iron rod might strike a stone and touch off the powder, but the inevitable happened.

The explosion blew the heavy iron rod up like a bullet. The point struck Gage in the cheekbone and the rod went up through his skull. It stopped with about eighteen inches of the tamping iron sticking out the crown of his head, the other end projecting downward from the left cheekbone. The pressure on the left eye was forcing it almost out of its socket.

In spite of his fearful injury, Gage did not lose consciousness. The blast threw him backward a couple of steps and he fell on his back, but he was only dazed for a few minutes. Fellow workmen got him to the nearest place where they could summon aid, a hotel about a mile from the scene of the accident; and upon arrival Gage got out of the conveyance without assistance and walked up a long flight of stairs to the doctor's office, where his wounds were given emergency treatment. There the iron rod was withdrawn and bits of bone and brain tissue were removed by a surgeon who had been called in. Neither of the doctors expected him to live, although he was fully conscious at ten o'clock on the night of the accident.

Phineas Gage recovered uneventfully. He lost the sight of his left eye, a small price to pay for his brush with death. Gage lived many years after the accident and was examined by numerous medical authorities of the day, none of whom could understand how a man could survive such a head injury.

At St. Vincent's Hospital in New York City in 1935 a baby was born with no brain whatever. Yet for twenty-seven days, in defiance of all medical concepts, the baby lived and ate and cried just like any other. In fact, the child's reactions were so normal that its true condition was not suspected until an autopsy disclosed the absence of a brain.

Drs. Gould and Pyle also report the case of a man who suffered from a brain tumor. Although the ailment had created a cavity in the brain almost five inches in length, the victim was possessed of all his faculties right up to the moment of his death.

In the book *From the Conscious to the Unconscious,* Dr. Gustave Geley has recorded the case of a young girl whose brain was crushed to a pulp by a railway accident; yet after a minimum of surgery she recovered fully and quickly.

In September of 1957 two doctors made a remarkable report to the American Psychological Association. Dr. Jan W. Bruell and Dr. George W. Albee told the organization that they had performed an operation in which they found it necessary to remove the entire right half of the patient's brain.

The patient in this case was a 39-year-old man of more than average intelligence, said the doctors. To their amazement he made a routine recovery after the drastic surgery and, they added, "The operation left his intellectual capacity virtually unimpaired."

Dr. Augustin Iturricha made an address before the Anthropological Society at Sucre, Bolivia, in 1940, and he left his colleagues with a question which has never been answered.

He and Dr. Nicholas Ortiz had studied at great length the case of a fourteen-year-old boy who had been a patient at the clinic of Dr. Ortiz. The boy was being treated for an abscess of the brain. He was fully conscious and rational up to the moment of death, complaining only of a violent headache. When the doctors conducted an autopsy on him, they discovered to their amazement that the boy was virtually decapitated. The brain mass was almost entirely detached from the bulb. There was a large abscess involving all of the cerebellum and part of the cerebrum.

Under these circumstances, what did he think with?

The puzzle which confronted Drs. Ortiz and Iturricha was no more baffling than that which the noted German brain specialist, Hufeland, recounts. He too may have had to revise some of his ideas when he performed an autopsy on the body of a paralyzed man who had been in full possession of his faculties to the last.

Instead of brains he had only eleven ounces of water.

16

The Mentalist
Who Solved Murders

Mass murder was almost unheard of in the quiet farming community of Mannville, Alberta, (Canada) in 1928. Yet, it had happened and the grisly evidence had been found on the farm of wealthy Henry Booher, about five miles from the town.

The family physician, Dr. Harley Heaslip, called the Royal Canadian Mounted Police and made the report of the murders to Constable Fred Olsen, who left immediately for the scene of the crimes.

It was a weird spectacle that confronted the officer and the doctor. As they entered the house they found the owner of the farm, Henry Booher, and his twenty-one-year-old son, Vernon, sitting at one side of the dining room table, staring across it at the body of Mrs. Booher. She was slumped over the table, face down, shot through the back of the head. The father and son were evidently in a state of shock, so Dr. Heaslip and Constable Olsen said nothing. The doctor beckoned the officer to follow him into the adjoining kitchen.

There was the corpse of Fred Booher, brother of Vernon,

sprawled on his back in a pool of blood. Fred had been shot in the face three times. Olsen theorized that the man had heard the shooting in the house and had been slain as he came to investigate.

"The mother and the eldest son," said Dr. Heaslip. "The others are out here, Constable."

In a barn behind the house they examined the body of William Roysk, killed by shots in the face. And the fourth victim of this orgy of murder, a hired hand named Gabe Goromby, lay sprawled grotesquely in a blood-spattered bunkhouse. He, too, had been shot in the face repeatedly.

There was no trace of the gun which had been used.

Constable Olsen made some notes on the killings and from the evidence he decided that Mrs. Booher, who had been shot in the back of the head, had been the first to die and was in reality the killer's intended target. The others, her eldest son and the two hired men, Olsen reasoned, had been shot down when they recognized the murderer. There was no attempt at burglary, so the crime was one of passion rather than plunder.

The Mountie went back to the house to question the badly shaken father. He confirmed what twenty-one-year-old Vernon had told the doctor during his almost incoherent phone call. Father and son had left the house after supper to work on different parts of the farm. The two daughters had gone to a basketball game. The elder brother, Fred, and the two hired men, were all working within earshot of the house. When Henry Booher had last seen his wife she was standing at the kitchen sink, just beginning the task of washing the dishes from the evening meal. Vernon said he had returned to the house about 8:30 p.m., had found the bodies of his mother and brother and had immediately phoned the doctor. He said he had not found the bodies of the hired men.

Constable Olsen concluded that the time Vernon mentioned checked with something else the officer had noted. At the time of her sudden death, Mrs. Booher had gone into the dining room and was picking stems from a pan of strawberries. Therefore, she had been shot before her son, Fred, was slain, for she certainly would not have been sitting there while the shooting was going on in the next room.

It was all very strange, thought the Constable. He idly dunked his hand in the soapy dishwater standing in the sink, water in which the dead woman had left a skillet soaking. Olsen felt something hard and sharp in the pan and brought it up. It was an empty cartridge case from a .303 rifle. The killer had carefully picked up all his cartridge cases . . . but this one he had overlooked. It might trap him.

Certainly the Boohers did not own, and had not owned, a rifle to fit that cartridge. A quick check, however, revealed that a nearby neighbor had owned a .303, but claimed that it had been stolen recently. Olsen made a note of the matter. Local police records showed that the owner of the rifle had indeed reported its theft, just as he claimed. Was it a move to cover a premeditated crime, Olsen wondered? A microscopic comparison of shells which had been fired from the "stolen" rifle matched the firing pin impression on the shell Olsen had recovered from Booher's sink. The missing weapon was the murder weapon. Find the man who had taken the gun from the neighbor's house and you find the killer, the Constable told himself.

The Mountie's problem was complicated by the sudden

realization that Vernon Booher had a poorly-concealed loathing for him. Time after time Olsen would turn quickly and catch young Booher sneering behind his back or glaring at him with looks steeped in hatred. On one such occasion, a week after the murders, Olsen asked Vernon the first question that came into his mind:

"Vernon, why don't you have a girl?"

The young man was taken aback but he managed to stammer: "I don't like girls!"

Why didn't he like girls? Olsen soon learned that Vernon had been dating a very pretty lass in nearby Mannville but the girl had given him the gate about six months before Olsen questioned her. She told the officer that Mrs. Booher had kept telling Vernon that she was immoral and that he was a fool to waste his time with her. Little by little, said the girl, she could see that Vernon was being influenced by his mother's accusations; so she had told him to stay away and not come back, that she didn't want to see him again.

"And did you go out with him any more after that?"

"No, indeed. And he was sorry, too!"

When Constable Olsen confronted Vernon Booher with the charge that he had hated his mother for breaking up his love affair, Vernon sneered at him and laughed. The officer repeated the accusation and added, "You killed your mother and then you killed the others, to keep them quiet!"

Young Booher showed no emotion. "Have you found the rifle?"

"No."

"Well, then," the young man said calmly, "how do you expect to convict anyone, especially me? You will certainly never get a confession out of me, you know."

Olsen felt that he had the killer but proving it in court

was something else again. Vernon Booher was taken to Provincial Police Headquarters at Edmonton, where veteran Inspector Hancock told the boy he might as well confess.

"That's what you think!" Vernon laughed, haughtily. Day after day the prisoner played cat-and-mouse with the authorities. They knew they could never get a conviction unless they could get a confession and, after a week, they were no nearer a confession than when they began. They had one chance—just one—to wring a confession from this icy-veined suspect—they had to find that murder weapon and prove that he had had it in his hands.

Inspector Hancock was in the throes of quiet desperation when he chanced to read in the paper one evening the report of a so-called mind reader, Maximillian Langsner, of Vancouver, who claimed to be able to solve crimes by reading the thoughts of criminals. For fear of ridicule, Hancock did not discuss his move with his associates; he just phoned Langsner to come ahead and show what he could do, if anything.

When the mentalist hopped off the train a couple of days later, he turned out to be a dapper little fellow, of thirty-five, who bore a remarkable resemblance to the actor Adolphe Menjou. He strutted up to Inspector Hancock and said, by way of introduction:

"You think I am a fraud and you have turned to me because you are desperate."

Hancock chuckled. "You don't have to be a mind reader to figure that out!"

As they made their way to the Mountie's office, the mentalist told the veteran officer the story of how he had been born in Vienna and had studied mental telepathy in the Orient. He claimed that the human mind, under stress, sends out signals which can be received and understood by other minds which are trained to the task.

Langsner said that he could sit down outside a prisoner's cell, as he professed to have done in Berlin, and wait for the prisoner to reveal the things that were hidden in his mind. In the Berlin case, he told Hancock, the prisoner had finally signaled the location of some stolen jewels, which police then recovered from Langsner's description of the place.

Was he just another screwball? Inspector Hancock was beginning to have misgivings about this gabby little dude who was boasting of such incredible exploits.

"Look," said the Mountie, "I've got to know what this suspect did with a certain type of rifle which was used to kill four people. Without the rifle we have no confession and without the confession we have no case."

"Then you want me to find out where the rifle is hidden. Is that right?"

"Exactly."

"Very simple, sir. If the rifle is important to you, it is even more important to him. If it is important to him, then he has to think about it. If he thinks about it, I can pick up the impulses sent out by his brain and interpret them for you. Eventually, he will tell us what you want to know!"

"Eventually? What do you mean by that?"

"I mean that sooner or later they all break. They may fuss and fidget and fume, but they know that I'm going to read their minds, sooner or later. Shall we visit our friend now? I am anxious to get started."

Shortly after lunch, Langsner took a folding chair out of Inspector Hancock's office and carried it into the jail and down the corridor to Booher's cell. He sat down, facing the cell, and began staring at the prisoner.

After three hours of this uninterrupted staring, Booher had lost his calm. He could no longer ignore this dandy with the gold-headed cane who sat there staring at him without saying a word. Booher tried to stare back. Then he began to mutter curses. Langsner just stared.

At the end of the fourth hour, Booher leaped up from his cot and charged to the bars. Sweat was dripping down his face. "I don't know who you are!" he shouted, "but get away from here, God damn you! Get away, I say!"

The owlish little man on the chair never changed expression. He just stared and blew smoke rings from his cigarette toward the frenzied prisoner.

The murder suspect flung himself back on his cot and turned his back on his silent tormentor. Inspector Hancock opened the door a crack to see how things were going. Langsner hastily scribbled a few words on a scrap of paper, rolled it into a ball and flipped it with his thumb to a point where Hancock could reach it without coming into the corridor.

The note said: "I will have him soon, like a fish on a string. Stay away."

The strange duel continued for another forty minutes. Then Booher slowly rose to a sitting position on the edge of the cot and twisted around to face Langsner. This was the moment the mentalist had been waiting for. His prey was mentally exhausted, open for inspection.

Inspector Hancock recorded that it was exactly five hours from the time that Langsner had begun his strange vigil that he opened the door of the Inspector's office wearing a smugly satisfied grin.

"Any results?"

"Of course. He told me mentally where that gun is hidden. I have a clear picture of a rifle hidden in a clump of bushes about five or six hundred feet from the farmhouse where the murders were done. Let me have a pencil and paper."

Langsner sat down at Hancock's desk and sketched out a farmhouse. Beyond the farmhouse was a clump of bushes. Halfway between the bushes and the house was a tree; beyond the bushes, another tree. He sketched only a portion of the house itself, but Hancock noticed that it was identical to the part nearest the clump of bushes, even to the peculiar scroll work around the eaves. The mentalist told Hancock that the house was white, with red shutters. This description fit the Booher house but was *not* like that of the neighbor who claimed the rifle had been stolen.

It was dusk when Inspector Hancock, Langsner and Constable Olsen arrived at the Booher farm. They looked at the drawing and at the house and had no trouble recognizing the place. Beyond it, a couple of hundred yards away across a field, were the trees and the clump of bushes just as Langsner had drawn them.

"That's the place!" Langsner exclaimed. "There are the bushes where the rifle is hidden!" He began to run across the field with the officers trailing a few yards behind him. The mentalist plunged into the bushes, swishing them about as he explored the soil, and suddenly he dropped on his knees and dug in the soft loam with both hands. By the time the police reached him he was holding aloft a .303 Enfield.

Needless to say, Hancock and Olsen were dumbfounded by this development. But their jubilation was tempered by the subsequent discovery that there were no usable finger-prints on the weapon. Vernon Booher was still not linked with the gun that had been used to murder four persons.

Inspector Hancock hurried back to the jail and confronted young Booher with the gun. The suspect was shaken but still capable of resistance. He refused to identify the weapon—said he had never seen it before.

"Sorry, son," said Hancock, "but you *have* seen it before. We found it right where you hid it and it has your finger-prints on it."

He was told how the police had found the gun through Langsner's picture of its hiding place, which the mentalist said Booher's mind has projected. Then Booher was taken back to the scene of the slayings. With his grief-stricken father and sisters facing him as silently as Langsner had done, Vernon Booher broke down and confirmed what the authorities had suspected. He blamed his mother for breaking up his love affair with the young lady in Mannville and said his hatred for her was so intense that he stole the rifle to kill her. The shot that murdered his mother brought Fred into the house, and he, too, became a victim. The hired men saw the killer come out of the house with the rifle, so they too were tracked down and slaughtered. Then Vernon wiped the rifle and hid it in the bushes before he called Doctor Heaslip.

Vernon Booher died on the gallows for his infamous butchery. Langsner was paid for his strange services by Inspector Hancock and was last heard of shortly before the outbreak of World War II when he left for a tour of the Middle East.

The case records of the mass murders at the Booher farm are on file with the Royal Canadian Mounted Police and the part played by Maximillian Langsner is a part of that record. Langsner's role was fully reported by the newspapers, thanks to Inspector Hancock, who had the facts and the courage to make them public.

17

Dr. Mitchell's Mystery

The late Dr. S. Weir Mitchell of Philadelphia was one of the most distinguished and respected members of his profession. His long career included being president of the American Association of Physicians and president of the American Neurological Society, honors given in tribute to his eminence and integrity. It is this background which makes his experience the more credible, and difficult to dismiss.

The last patient had left his office about ten-thirty in the evening of what had been a long and tiring day for Dr. Mitchell. With a sigh of relief, the aging physician hung up his stethoscope, turned off the gas light in his waiting room and went across the hall into the kitchen of his home for a glass of milk.

A few minutes later when he checked his front door to make certain that it was locked he noticed that the thick fleecy snow flakes were still swirling down and were inches deep on the sidewalk in front of his house. Dr. Mitchell dimmed the gas light in the front hall and trudged wearily upstairs to his bedroom.

Half an hour later, as he lay there reading a book, the

front door bell jangled—or was he hearing things? A moment later it jangled again, more insistently this time. Perhaps whoever it was would go away if he didn't answer it. But what if it was an emergency involving one of his patients, several of whom were seriously ill at their homes? He had little choice but to slip into his robe and slippers and make his way downstairs again, tired as he was.

When he opened the front door he discovered that the young girl who stood there was a total stranger. She was thinly dressed for such a night, he noticed; no coat, just the conventional high button shoes, a heavy green woolen dress and a flimsy gray plaid shawl over her head and gathered under the chin with a blue glassy-looking clasp. The doctor quickly guessed that she was from a poor section of the city, down the hill a few blocks from his house.

"Won't you come in out of the snow, please?"

The girl stepped just inside the door.

"My mother is very ill," she said. "She needs you right away, sir. Please come with me!"

Dr. Mitchell hesitated. Here was a total stranger and in all probability a charity case, asking him to go out into a snow storm at the end of a day that had left him exhausted. He was not eager to make the trip.

"Don't you have a family doctor, my child?"

She shook her head and snow fell from the shawl.

"No, sir. And my mother is dreadfully ill, doctor! Please come with me! Please do! Now!"

Her pinched white face—the unmistakable note of urgency in her voice—the tears that were beginning to well up in her eyes—forced Dr. Mitchell not to refuse her. He asked her to be seated while he dressed, but she said she preferred to stand. He hurried upstairs.

A few moments later, with the girl leading the way down the hill as he had expected, the oddly assorted pair made their way through the storm. Doctor Mitchell knew the neighborhood for which they were headed—it was one in which low paid factory workers lived from payday to payday, and eked out the barest of existences, for the most part. He had made many trips into that community during his career; one more wasn't going to hurt him— and it might save a life.

The girl never spoke after they left his house. She walked along two or three steps in front of him in the soft snow without looking back. At last she turned into a narrow areaway between two ramshackle houses that were virtual tenements. With the doctor close behind her she felt her way up a dark stairway and to the end of a dingy hall where the yellow glow of an oil lamp shone through a transom. The girl opened the door softly and stepped aside as Dr. Mitchell entered.

Poverty was master here. A badly worn carpet that covered only the center of the splintery floor, a tin cupboard in one corner, a sheet metal upright stove with no fire in it. And on the bed in the corner of the room lay a middle-aged woman struggling for her breath. Dr. Mitchell went to work.

The patient had pneumonia and as the girl had said, she was very, very ill. Under the circumstances there was not much that Dr. Mitchell could do except to give her some emergency medication. He would certainly have to call again tomorrow. He noted with relief that the woman was conscious—that would help.

The doctor looked around for the girl who had brought him to this place. A fire would have to be built—this woman could not fight her ailment in a cold room. Then it occurred to Dr. Mitchell that he had not seen the girl since he entered the room. He looked around again. The door of a shabby chiffonier stood open. There were the garments the girl had worn a few minutes before—the heavy dress, the hightop shoes—the gray shawl with the blue glass pin still dangling from it. When had the child changed clothes, with the doctor right there in the room?

He stepped over to the chiffonier and looked closely at the garments—the sick woman following his movements with her eyes. Dr. Mitchell touched the shoes and the shawl. They were dry!

"Those are my daughter's clothes," the woman gasped.

"Yes, I know," said Dr. Mitchell. "But where is your daughter? I must talk to her."

There was a long silence. Slowly the sick woman turned to face him, her eyes swimming with tears.

"Talk to her? Doctor, she died two months ago!"

18

Gilbert Stuart's
Prophetic Picture

Gilbert Stuart, the noted portrait painter, is world famous for his painting of George Washington. It was one of many fine works that he produced during his long and brilliant career—a career which included an assignment from Lord Mulgrave that had a most unusual sequel.

Mulgrave's brother, General Phipps, was soon to be assigned to service in India, and his Lordship wanted a picture of the General before he left for that dangerous outpost. Gilbert Stuart received the commission for the portrait, which he duly executed. Since he knew and liked both Mulgrave and Phipps, Stuart gave more time and attention to detail than he might have done otherwise.

At last the picture was finished and it was delivered to Lord Mulgrave. When it was unveiled in his parlor, his Lordship was taken aback.

"Good God! What is this? What is the meaning of this? This is very strange!"

"I have painted your brother exactly as I saw him," the artist explained.

Lord Mulgrave shook his head sadly. "I see insanity in that face," he muttered.

General Phipps reached India on schedule, but the first account Lord Mulgrave had of him was that the General had committed suicide . . . . . in a fit of insanity.

19

The Case Of The
Psychic Detective

In the *Milwaukee* (Wisconsin) *News* of November 6, 1935, there was considerable space devoted to the astounding prediction which had been made by a local man, Arthur Price Roberts, on October 18th of that same year. Roberts, then nearly seventy years old and famed for his abilities as a "psychic detective," had warned the Milwaukee police that there was violence just ahead. Said Roberts: "Going to be lots of bombings—dynamitings! I see two banks blown up and perhaps the city hall. Going to blow up police stations. Then there's going to be a big blow-up south of the river (Menomonee) and then it'll all be over!"

Roberts made those predictions to a Detective English and others who were well aware of his strange talents. As a result, extra precautions were taken and patrols were increased.

Eight days after Roberts' warning the first blast came. It was a dynamite blast that tore to bits the village hall in suburban Shorewood. Two children were killed, scores of persons injured, the debris gutted by fire. On October 27th, the dynamiters struck at two Milwaukee banks, just as Roberts had predicted, and as a supreme gesture of defiance two police stations were shattered with bombs. Harried police were without clues and the helpless city waited for the next blow.

Where would it fall?

Since Doc Roberts had correctly predicted the explosions up to that moment, it was only natural that the police should go to him. Detective English and his superior officers asked Robert what they should expect.

"On Sunday, November 4th, there'll be a big one south of the Menomonee. And that'll be all!"

Could he identify or describe the perpetrators of these outrages? Doc was sorry—but he could only tell them what he had already told them.

The Milwaukee police sent a small army of men into the Menomonee district. Every man was fully armed, all were deadly marksmen, and all were instructed to shoot first and ask questions later if the circumstances indicated definitive action. The bombers must be stopped.

On the afternoon of Sunday, November 4th, Milwaukee was jarred to its foundations by a thunderous explosion. Residents eight miles away heard it and ran out to see what had happened.

It took some patient and grisly police work to determine the events leading up to that sixth and final explosion. The garage where it had been centered was obliterated by the fury of the explosion. A sackful of bits of human flesh, scattered over several blocks, was carefully collected. Did they belong to the bombers, or to the victims?

Bit by bit, the story was pieced together.

Hugh Rutkowski, twenty-one, and his buddy, nineteen-year-old Paul Chovonee, had died when the fifty pounds of dynamite they were fashioning into their sixth bomb accidentally detonated.

Roberts had correctly predicted the entire series of explosions, including the final blast, which was accidental.

For him, and for the police of Milwaukee and other communities who sought his assistance, it was an old and familiar story.

Since his childhood in Denbeigh, Wales, where he was born in 1866, Arthur Roberts, also known as "Doc," had shown an uncanny faculty of being able to locate missing persons and objects and, as in the case of the Milwaukee bombings, of foreseeing events with surprising clarity. He remained an illiterate all his life because he was fearful that education would destroy his strange ability. As news of his inexplicable talents spread, the little office he maintained in his home was filled with mementos of his successes, accumulated over a period of fifty years.

Not all that he did is in those records, for on many assignments Roberts worked with authorities on a highly confidential basis. One such case was that of a convicted murderer, Ignatz Potz, of Chicago. Relatives of Potz sought help from Roberts. With only a few hours remaining before execution, Potz received a commutation of his sentence to life imprisonment—the result of evidence uncovered with the aid of Doc Roberts. Roberts found evidence which indicated that Potz had told the truth about some aspects of the killing, although he had been unable to support his statements.

In July of 1905, Duncan McGregor of Pestigo, Wisconsin, suddenly vanished. Rewards were offered, countless false clues were run to earth—and McGregor was still miss-

94

ing. As the months dragged by without a trace of her missing husband, Mrs. McGregor decided to seek help from the illiterate "psychic detective"—Doc Roberts. When she walked up to the door of his home in Milwaukee, she told friends, Roberts met her at the door, correctly identified her and the nature of her mission. He also told her that he could not give her any information beyond what she already had, but asked her to come back in a few hours, after he had had time to think about the case.

Roberts told police that in this case he failed to get the mental flash that usually came to his aid, so he decided to lie down, go into a sort of trance, and see if that method would help.

It did.

When Mrs. McGregor returned that afternoon, Roberts told her that her husband had been murdered . . . "but," he added, "I cannot tell you who was responsible for his death. The testimony I could give you would not be admissible evidence in court. I would only be troubling myself to give it."

Roberts then proceeded to describe to Mrs. McGregor a spot in the Menomonee River where he claimed her husband's body was located. It was unable to rise to the surface because it was snagged in some sunken logs, he said. A few hours later, police authorities found the spot Roberts had described and brought up the body of the missing man, after untangling the clothing from some sunken logs.

Another case concerned J. D. Leroy, a wealthy Chicago businessman, trying to find his brother, who had gone to Albuquerque and had not been heard from in six months. Roberts told him the brother had been murdered and gave a detailed description of the spot in Devil's Canyon, Arizona, where he said the body would be found. Three weeks later Mr. J. D. Leroy wrote to Roberts to thank him for his help. The letter said that the body of the missing man, a murder victim, was found in Devil's Canyon about two hundred feet from the spot described by Roberts.

What was perhaps one of the most dramatic of Doc Roberts' strange cases was that which began while he was staying at a Fond du Lac hotel.

There had been an unsolved murder there two years before, and local police authorities, knowing of his fantastic background, asked him if he could provide them with any leads. Without hesitation, Doc closed his eyes, leaned back in his rocking chair and began to describe the victim with remarkable accuracy. But that was as far as he could get. He asked the police to let him sleep on it.

The skeptics snickered, of course. Doc had told them nothing they had not already known. But next morning he walked into the police station, asked to see the file of pictures from the rogue's gallery. Thumbing through them quickly until he came to some photographs of cheap stick-up men, Doc put his finger on one and said:

"There's your killer, gentlemen! You will find him in British Columbia — working for the Mounted Police Service!"

And once again, Doc was right.

His strange talents, whatever they were, led Doc into some exciting experiences. When a taxi driver named Fred Kores was slugged, thrown out of his cab, and had his car stolen near Racine, Wisconsin, the owner of the cab company, Warren Boucher, asked Roberts for help.

Twenty-four hours later Roberts rushed into Boucher's office.

"I've located your car," he exclaimed. "but you'll have to hurry before the thief gets away!"

Boucher and Roberts scrambled into the front seat of Boucher's car; Kores, the taxi driver, and a friend got into the rear seat. Following the directions given by the agitated Roberts they drove to an intersection south of Cudahy, on the road to Chicago. Roberts asked them to stop the car while he got his bearings, frankly admitting that he was confused. He got out of the car, paced nervously along the roadside for a moment and then jumped back into the automobile.

"Go that way!" he exclaimed, pointing down a side road.

Their car had proceeded less than a quarter of a mile when Roberts shouted: "The car is coming toward us! Turn around and we'll follow it!"

At the moment several cars were approaching, all of them moving rapidly and at least a couple of hundred yards distant. Boucher cut sharply into a driveway, turned around and just then a car shot past them. Kores, the taxi driver who had been slugged and robbed, yelled: "That's it, Warren! That's my cab and that's the guy who slugged me!"

Once again the inexplicable instincts of old Doc Roberts were right in every respect. Boucher forced the other car off the road, his companions seized the driver, and Milwaukee police got his confession to the robbery and the theft.

Arthur Price Roberts, the illiterate psychic detective, was seventy-three years old and apparently in excellent health when he attended a little dinner party in his honor in November of 1939. As the gathering began to break up Doc thanked the group for the honor they had paid him and for the wonderful association he had had with each and every one of them down through the years.

Then he said: "You know how much I enjoy these meetings of ours but I am afraid that I won't be present at the next one you are talking about. As much as I would like to remain, I won't be with you beyond January 2, 1940."

His prediction was correct in every detail.

On January 2, 1940, he died quietly in his modest little home in Milwaukee, surrounded by file cabinets filled with documents attesting to his remarkable career. What he had done is a matter of record, but how he did it remains an unsolved riddle.

PART
TWO

20

Mathematical Master Minds

In 1940, when he was sixteen and already well known for his remarkable mental feats, Willis Dysart was hired as a special election night feature by an aggressive Minnesota newspaper. Their problem was how to assemble and present the torrent of election returns in order to keep ahead of their competitors—and as it turned out, they made the correct choice in hiring Willis.

He was one of that small, select group of unusual persons known as mathematical marvels. He had been investigated by many psychologists and mathematicians, not with the idea of exposing any possible trickery, for none existed, but with a view to learning how far his abilities went and, if possible, how he had acquired them. As in all other such cases the medics and mathematicians went away acknowledging his powers without understanding their nature.

On that 1940 election night young Willis Dysart stood before a battery of microphones and rattled off the incoming returns as fast as they were handed to him. He could instantly give the exact standing of any candidate on the board, including his current total, the percentage of votes counted at that point and the probable outcome of the contest on the basis of existing information. Needless to say, the paper that hired Willis that night scored some memorable scoops over all competitors who were forced to rely on adding machines and ordinary calculators.

For the gifted young man at the microphone it was a routine performance. To break the monotony of giving election returns and their projections, Willis had the editors give him the birth dates of the various candidates. He would instantly reply, giving the years, months, hours, minutes and seconds the candidate had lived to that moment. Even this was no real problem to a man who could multiply any given seven digit number by any six-digit number in five seconds or less.

As a practical matter, a building contractor who was authorized to construct a large schoolhouse, once asked Willis to tell him how many bricks he would need for the structure. He gave Willis the dimensions, the number and size of windows and doors and stone trim, and in seven seconds Willis wrote down the answer. When the building was finished the contractor found that he had one-half a brick left over.

Willis Dysart had little schooling and no training in figures beyond simple arithmetic. His family attested to the truth of his claim that the only book he had ever read in its entirety was the Bible.

When she was nineteen years old in 1951, Shakuntali Devi was brought to the United States to repeat the dazzling feats of mental mathematics with which she had astounded the scholars of India and London. A slight, shy girl whose speech was so soft it was almost inaudible, she did not disappoint anyone.

For her, these public exhibitions of mental wizardry with figures was an old, old story. She gave the first demonstration of her ability to deal rapidly with huge sums and complicated problems when she was only six years old. She was one of twelve children in a family which lived in a small village near Bangalore, India. Her childhood ability to multiply big numbers by other big numbers in a matter of seconds brought her considerable publicity and she was much in demand for schools and political gatherings. It was incredible that this tiny girl with the big dark eyes could simply stand there in the middle of the platform, listen to a request for six or seven figures to be multiplied by another number of similar length and give the correct answer in a matter of three or four seconds. Yet she did it innumerable times and the judges always had to wait for the mathematicians to punch out their versions of the same problem on their calculating machines.

As she grew older Shakuntali lost interest in the feats of multiplication which had won her so much acclaim. She gradually dropped that part of her performance entirely as being too easy, and went in for more difficult feats. She considers finding the square root of numbers with several digits such child's play that she refuses to bother with it. But cube roots? Shakuntali delights in beating the machines to the answer, as she did in the case where the problem was to find the cube root of 332,812,557. In exactly two-fifths of a second she had written out the correct answer —693. It was just one of the many demonstrations where she had only to glance at a perfect number up to nine figures to produce the fourth root; she could, and *did,* give practically instantaneous answers in providing the sixth root of figures with as many as twelve digits.

Although she is a show piece in the field of mathematics, Shakuntali Devi has difficulties with the rest of her studies and twice failed in her intermediate examination when she studied for her B.A. degree.

How does she make such intricate calculations in her mind with such fantastic speed? Shakuntali says she does not know, but she knows that it requires constant practice or she seems to lose the knack. She has a younger sister who once showed signs of developing into a mathematical genius too, but lack of interest cost her the gift.

In an earlier book (*Stranger Than Science*, 1959) I discussed the mathematical wizardry of the noted slave, Old Tom Fuller, an illiterate who could nevertheless perform such feats as multiplying one nine-digit number by another. Like Miss Devi, he seemed to do it by intuition and almost instantaneously. Among those who came to this prodigy for use of his strange powers was George Washington, who had Tom calculate for him the value of a tobacco crop and the number of fish of a certain size that could be stowed in a boat that belonged to a neighbor.

Another mathematical genius was Zerah Colburn, a native of New England, who went to London in 1814 when he was ten years old and gave public exhibitions of his wizardry, which included raising eight to the sixteenth power. He produced the correct answer, 281,474,976,710,656 —in slightly more than one minute. He could tell square roots instantly and amazed the most learned men of Europe with his mental prowess. But as he grew older and broadened his education, his ability to perform declined and was finally reduced to little more than normal.

104

Jacques Inaudi, who was born in 1867, was illiterate until he was twenty years of age, yet at the age of seven he was giving public demonstrations of such feats as finding the cube and even fifth roots of numbers and of subtracting in less than two seconds twenty-one digits from another figure of the same length. Inaudi differed from his fellow wizards in that he talked to himself continually as he worked. He said he did not see the answers in his mind—but heard them as he muttered.

Jedediah Buxton (1702-1772) was also illiterate and was unquestionably stupid as well. But his ability to juggle huge sums in his head was unsurpassed, and he could solve fantastic problems while he carried on conversations with fellow laborers.

The illiterate Sicilian shepherd, Vito Mangiamele, appeared before the Paris Academy of Sciences at ten. When he was asked to name the number, whose cube is plus five times its square, and which is equal to four times itself increased by forty, Vito blinked and replied "five." Then the scientists blinked.

A genius with numbers and a near-idiot otherwise was the noted Johann Dase of Hamburg, 1824-1861. He could tell at a glance the number of books on a shelf or the number of peas spilled on a table. He did not understand the simplest mathematical proposition, yet because of his unequalled feats he drew a mathematical research grant for many years. Perhaps his outstanding demonstration was to multiply a one hundred digit number by another of the same size, mentally, in eight hours and forty-five minutes.

Mental mathematicians are rather more numerous than is generally realized.

The American T. H. Safford (1836-1901) is usually

listed among outstanding astronomers of his time, yet he was equally as noted for his feats of mental calculation. At nine he computed and published an almanac, using new rules for calculating eclipses. At ten he was asked to multiply two fifteen-digit numbers and gave the fantastic thirty-six digit answer in fifty-eight seconds.

The noted scientist Gauss (1777-1855) was not only the greatest mathematician of his century but he was also a noted mental calculator at a very early age. When he was only three years old he startled his father by pointing out an error in the parent's calculations. Famed for his discoveries in the field of magnetism, Gauss is virtually unknown today for his spectacular feats in mathematics.

George Bidder, 1806-1878, was probably the best known of the British boy wonders. He was the son of a poverty stricken stonecutter and when he first showed his amazing calculating ability at the age of six his father promptly took him on tour, a venture from which he was rescued by admirers who recognized the value of his talents. George was sent to Edinburgh University where he won the mathematics prize in 1822. When he was twelve, a group of professors asked him for the answer to this one: If a pendulum swings nine and three-quarter inches in one second, how many inches will it swing in seven years, fourteen days, two hours, one minute and fifty-six seconds—counting each year as three hundred and sixty-five days, five hours, forty minutes and fifty seconds? In less than one minute George had given them the answer—2,165,625,744¾ inches.

The professors asked him how he got the answer so quickly and George replied: "Well, Sir, you said the years were all the same length so I figured it out for one year and multiplied by seven. Then I figured it out for the months, days, hours, minutes and seconds. It was rather easy that way."

Easy, perhaps, if you happened to have the mind of a George Bidder, who went on from being a boy wonder in mathematics to one of the world's greatest civil engineers, for whom the Victoria Docks still stand as a memorial after his feats of mental calculation have been largely forgotten.

21

Murder On His Mind

The little theater at Beechy, Saskatchewan, (Canada), was crowded on the night of December 10, 1932. In the audience was Constable Carey, an officer of the Royal Canadian Mounted Police. He was not there in an official capacity, but had come to be entertained by the featured performer, a tall, grey-haired, handsome fellow who billed himself as "Professor Gladstone, Mentalist."

After that night's performance, life was never quite the same for Constable Carey.

The show offered the usual bit of "mind-reading" and the customary act of hypnotizing volunteers from the audience who went through some amusing antics to the delight of the crowd. Then Professor Gladstone dismissed the hypnosis volunteers and stood peering down into the front and center section of the audience.

"Don't move!" he exclaimed. "Everyone stay where you are, please!"

It was sheer dramatics, perhaps, for no one had any intention of moving and no one did. The mentalist came down the steps in the center of the stage, all the while staring intently at someone in that center section.

He stepped directly in front of Bill Taylor, a well-known local rancher. Gladstone stared fixedly at Taylor for a couple of seconds. The theater was quite silent.

"I have it!" Gladstone exclaimed. "Yes, I have it! You are thinking about your friend Scotty McLauchlin! . . . He was murdered! . . . Brutally and wantonly murdered! The snow was spattered with blood!"

The startled audience gasped in unison at this astounding pronouncement. Bill Taylor's face blanched. But Gladstone had finished with him. The mentalist swung to face the Mounted Police officer a few seats from Taylor. He pointed his finger at Constable Carey.

"That's him! That's the man!"

All eyes were upon the startled officer. Carey gripped the arms of his seat. Was this man insane? What did he mean?

Gladstone continued, almost without pause.

"That's the man—in the red coat there! He is the one who will find the body of the murdered man. And I'll be with him when he does!"

The stunned audience was shocked into silence. They all knew Scotty McLauchlin, who had vanished one night in January nearly four years before. They knew that Scotty's disappearance was a mystery that remained unsolved. Now this strange man called it murder and proclaimed that Constable Carey would find the body. What did it all mean? How could such things be?

Actually, Gladstone had simply put into words, publicly, what everyone had long suspected. But Gladstone went further than anyone else had dared to do by claiming that he and Carey would find proof the slaying—the body of the victim.

Scotty McLauchlin had come to Beechy in 1919 and, with his congenial traits and contagious smile, had immediately made friends. For several years he had done well, but when his wife died, he turned his two children over to neighbors and began quarreling with two others of his neighbors about women. He was last seen alive on Sunday, January 16, 1929, when he visited with his friends. He told them that he had finished selling off what little he still owned and that he was taking the night train at nearby Herbert, to make a new try in British Columbia. Scotty invited his friends to see him off at Herbert, but those who went were disappointed; for Scotty failed to appear —and no one had seen him since.

Naturally, Constable Carey wanted to talk privately with this mentalist who had claimed publicly to know so much about the disappearance of Scotty McLauchlin. In Carey's office after the show, Gladstone reiterated his claims and could only explain them by saying that he "felt" that what he said was true—that he did it by extra-sensory perception which he could not otherwise explain—and that the power, whatever it was, had never misled him.

That night, still skeptical and somewhat confused, Carey called his superior, Detective Corporal Jack Woods of the Criminal Investigation Bureau in Saskatoon. Woods heard Carey's report with tongue in cheek; yet, as he listened, Woods realized that "Professor Gladstone" had them over a barrel. He might be nothing more than a publicity-seeker, a crackpot; yet now that he had declared himself publicly, the Mounties could do no less than give him a chance to make a fool of himself.

Woods told Carey to make an appointment with the mentalist for the following morning in Beechy. Pulling the three-year-old records on the McLauchlin case from the unsolved file, Corporal Woods reviewed the facts as he rode to the excited community.

Detective Corporal Woods later admitted that he was strangely impressed when Gladstone walked into Carey's office. The tall, dignified, grey-haired mentalist certainly did not appear to be a crackpot. Instead, he gave the impression of a man who was sure of himself and who was not playing pranks.

After Gladstone repeated the statements he had made in the theater the day before, he reviewed for the Mounties the murder scene which he had "observed" in his mind. He did not know the name of the killer, he said, but felt that he could identify him when he saw him, so vivid had been the impression of his mental experience which had re-created the alleged crime.

Both the officers realized that they had little evidence on which to proceed. They had questioned all the persons who had seen Scotty on the night he vanished and they had gotten nowhere. One of them, Jack Renton, had admitted that he and Scotty had quarreled over Yvonne Bourget, whom Jack had married shortly after Scotty's disappearance. But that was not evidence on which to hang a murder indictment.

The mentalist and the two officers piled into Wood's police car and began their rounds. Renton repeated the story he had told them before and the mentalist whispered that this was not the man. At the ramshackle house of a farmer named Si Young they heard that another rancher, named Schumacher, had threatened to kill Scotty—and the threats had been made in the presence of a fellow named Ed Vogel.

Vogel was suffering from lapse of memory when the officers found him. He was unquestionably disturbed and angry at being interrogated. The remark Si Young had attributed to him about Schumacher's threats were all lies, he snapped.

The officers had risen to leave when Gladstone stepped forward. He pointed his finger in Vogel's face.

"I'll tell you what happened, Vogel! You were sick in bed. Schumacher pushed through the door and told you he had had a quarrel with McLauchlin and swore that he would kill that damned Scotty before he was through with him!"

When Gladstone finished speaking, Vogel's face was blanched, his lips quivered, and he dropped into a chair. The mentalist bored in to attack again. He told Vogel why he had been in bed when Schumacher called—the minor but debilitating ailment that had laid him up for three days. Vogel nodded but did not look up.

The silence was broken a few seconds later by Vogel's white-faced chattering:

"You're right—you're right as hell about the whole thing! Schumacher did come to my place—like you said—cussed Scotty and swore that he'd kill that damned little Scotchman yet!"

At Schumacher's farm they were told by a farm hand that his boss had gone to town. The officers told the farm hand they were water-diviners (dowsers) from the Department of Agriculture and asked permission to tramp around the place. This was given. As they made their way over the snow-covered fields, Gladstone suddenly asked them to slow down. He explained that he felt nervous and disturbed.

"There's a disagreeable odor around here!"

Woods and Carey afterward said that they were not impressed with that observation since they always found disagreeable odors around a herd of cattle. Gladstone declared that he was near the body of Scotty McLauchlin but, if he was, the officers were unable to find it. They searched until it was nearly dark, without result, and when they were told that Schumacher still had not returned home they got into their car and started back to town. On the road they narrowly missed a collision with a big truck that was running without lights. Woods swung around and took up the pursuit. He forced the truck to stop and went back to arrest the driver, a huge blond fellow who turned out to be Schumacher. They took him back to town for questioning at the barracks.

For nearly an hour it was a calm repetition of what he had told them long before. McLauchlin, who had been Schumacher's partner on the farm had indicated a desire to sell out and Schumacher had paid him about one hundred and fifty dollars in cash and had given him a note for two hundred dollars for the balance. The police were getting nowhere.

Then Gladstone got up and paced nervously back and forth. Stopping before Schumacher, he turned to the suspect and snapped his fingers under the farmer's nose.

"It's the barn!" Gladstone croaked. "Now I can tell you how you did it! Scotty left the house to go to the barn and you followed him. You forced him into a quarrel—there was a fight! . . . Scotty fell like this . . ." Gladstone threw himself backward. "But you kept striking—and striking—until you knew he was dead! Then you buried his body near the barn—under some rubbish!"

Gladstone's sweaty red face was in marked contrast to the colorless countenance of Schumacher. The accused and the accuser stood staring at each other for a few seconds, then Schumacher recovered himself enough to tell the officers to go to hell and take Gladstone with them.

On the following morning, Schumacher was brought out of his cell and taken back to his farm. If the mentalist could produce the body of the missing man, Schumacher was certain to face a murder charge.

While two officers guarded Schumacher in the kitchen of his own house, Gladstone, Woods and Carey headed for the barn. Gladstone went right on through the structure and out the back door. Probing with his foot, he stopped at a frozen manure pile and turned to the officers.

"Scotty McLauchlin is buried under there, gentlemen."

Half a dozen farmers who had come to watch the proceedings grabbed picks and shovels and assaulted the heap, but it was slow going in the frozen soil and, after an hour of hard work with no results, they were ready to call a halt. Officer Woods went back to the house and suggested to Schumacher that he come out and show them where the body was buried. Schumacher refused to answer.

As Woods started back toward the barn to halt the digging, he was greeted with a shout. One of the farmers had brought up a dark woolen sock. A few moments later they had a skull, wrapped in a bloody scarf that some of them recognized as similar to the one Scotty always wore.

Mounted Police pathologists determined that they had indeed found the body of the missing Scotty McLauchlin, and found it under the condition that the mentalist had predicted. Further investigation disclosed that Schumacher had double-crossed Scotty on the rental of the farm and again after buying him out, and murdered him to get his money back. The body showed that Scotty had been beaten to death with a shovel. Schumacher, who could not write, finally broke down and confessed the crime. The stenographer's copy of what he said was almost a verbatim description of the slaying as Gladstone had pictured it to the police.

Schumacher was tried and convicted in the court at Kindersley and was sentenced to a long prison term, which he served at Prince Albert Penitentiary. Only a technicality saved him from the hangman's noose.

And what of Professor Gladstone? As a result of the widespread publicity given to the case of Scotty McLauchlin, he was much in demand and played for many years on the stage. But he was never again able to duplicate his performance at Beechy, Saskatchewan, on that bleak December night in 1932, when the mentalist solved a murder for the Royal Mounted Police.

22

Sleepless People

One of the most annoying discoveries
the medical profession ever made was the realization that
so many things it *knew* were false. For instance, there was
the old axiom that a person could exist without sleep just
about the same length of time that he could go without
food. Sleep, so the medical students are told, is food for
the brain. Starve the brain and you perish.

As late as the 1940's there lived a rugged old eccentric
named Al Herpin. He was then about ninety years old and
he resided in a tar paper shack on the outskirts of Trenton,
New Jersey. It was like many other shacks which served as
home to the homeless in Al Herpin's plane of existence—
except for one thing. His shack had no bed, no cot, not
even a hammock. And there was a good reason for the
omission. Al Herpin had never slept a wink in his life.

He was examined by scores of doctors who watched him
in relays for weeks on end, only to admit their bewilderment. They found that although he did not sleep, he did
not die either, as they had been led to believe he must. At
the age of ninety, Al had outlived many of the doctors who
had examined him, doctors who got their regular periods

of sleep. His mentality was above average, his health and appetite were good and Al worked at the various odd jobs he held to eke out an existence.

After a day's work he got tired, of course; but, since he was unable to sleep, Al Herpin would simply drop into his favorite chair, a broken-down rocker that he had rescued from the city dump, and read until he felt rested. After one of these pauses that refreshed, he was ready for work again.

Although the doctors who examined him could offer no explanation for his fantastic chronic insomnia, Al was inclined to agree with his mother, who had always held that his inability to sleep was the result of a severe injury she suffered a few days before he was born.

There have been others who suffered from this same condition. Among them was the well-known total insomniac, David Jones, of Anderson, Indiana, as reported in the local paper there on December 11, 1895:

"David Jones of this city, who attracted the attention of the entire medical profession two years ago by a sleepless spell of ninty-three days and last year by another spell which extended over one hundred and thirty-one days, is beginning on another which he feels will be more serious than the preceding ones. He was put on the circuit jury three weeks ago, and counting today he has not slept for twenty days and nights. He eats and talks as well as usual and is full of business and activity. He does not experience any bad effects whatever from the spell, nor did he during the one hundred and thirty-one days. During that spell he attended to all of his farm business. He says now that he feels as though he will never sleep again. He does not seem to bother himself about the prospects of a long and tedious wake. Mr. Jones cannot attribute his abnormality to any one thing but thinks it was probably superinduced by the use of tobacco while very young."

Unable to explain Mr. Jones as a fraud and unwilling to accept him as a fact, the medical profession left him alone.

He was followed on the records by a hapless housewife of Cegled, Hungary. Mrs. Rachel Sagi awakened one morning in 1911 with a splitting headache. It was so distressing that she visited the family doctor, who told her that she had been getting too much sleep. As ridiculous as it sounds, he may have been right. From that day forward until the time of her death in 1936, Mrs. Rachel Sagi never had another wink of sleep—a period of twenty-five years, two months and eleven days. She had no sleep, and no headaches.

One of the most recent cases of this sort to come to light is that of a Spanish farm laborer who walked into Madrid on the morning of November 29, 1960.

Valentin Medina, 61, had walked the entire one hundred and forty miles from southern Castille to Madrid in four days and four nights, "just resting a little by the roadside whenever my feet got to hurting."

Why had he made such a grueling trip?

Medina replied that he wanted the doctors at Provincial Hospital to examine him to see if they could cure his sleeplessness. He had come, he said, on the advice of his home-town doctor, after that gentleman had been unable to help him.

The medics at Provincial Hospital checked with Medina's home-town doctor, who confirmed that he had known the patient since childhood and that his own father, also a doctor, had treated Medina more than fifty years ago and had never known him to sleep a wink.

After lengthy tests at the hospital, the medics were convinced that he did not sleep. They were so impressed by his sincerity and his poverty that they arranged for him to return home by train, the first train ride he ever had.

Medina told newsmen: "I work like a beast. I never get tired of working. I still sign my name with my finger but I would like to know how to read and write. Nights would be shorter for me if I knew how to read books. All my life, while the rest of the world sleeps, I can only sit in front of the kitchen fireplace and wait till the rooster crows."

The doctors who examined him at Provincial Hospital sent him home with a prescription they compounded of several potent tranquilizers, in the hope that they might enable him to sleep for once in his life. Three weeks later they received a letter from Medina's own physician who thanked them for their kindness to his strange patient and who concluded by saying: "He has stopped taking the prescription you gave him. When he got tired his feet went to sleep—but he didn't."

In August of 1961, Eustace Burnett was eighty-one years old. He was a retired farmer living near Leicester, England. There was little to distinguish him from any other retired farmer of that community, except for the fact that Eustace never slept.

When he was twenty-seven years old, he lost the desire for sleep and in the ensuing fifty-four years he spent his nights reading books, listening to the radio or working crossword puzzles while the rest of the family got their rest.

Doctors came from afar to see for themselves that he really didn't sleep and that he enjoyed excellent health.

Of course the medics experimented with various means which normally produce sleep, but in the case of Mr. Burnett they were just wasting their time—and his. Hypnotism didn't even make him drowsy. Sleeping pills only gave him headaches.

After the medics had gone, Mr. Burnett went back to his normal routine . . . six hours in bed each night to rest his body, while his mind remained on duty, fully alert and active.

Eustace Burnett, like Valentin Medina, can truthfully say, "I never slept a wink last year!"

23

The Enchanted Pencil

One of the many fascinating architectural ruins of England is that of the famed Glastonbury Abbey, sometimes referred to as "the holiest spot in Britain." There was a legend that Jesus, in his young manhood, had come to Glastonbury with a relative, Joseph of Arimathea. One of the earliest historians of Britain, Gildas, who probably lived in the Sixth Century, says that Jesus came to Glastonbury for meditation in the last years of Tiberius Caesar—which would be not later than 27 A.D.

It is certain that as early as 597 A.D. St. Augustine wrote to Pope Gregory describing the impressive church which already existed at Glastonbury, and that the Doomsday Book, compiled by the minions of William the Conqueror about 1086, also mentions in detail the same magnificent structure. By 1086, the church had become a shrine to which the faithful made pilgrimages, and it had also become the burying place of kings, including King Arthur and his beloved Guinevere. Rising as it did from the surrounding marshes, it was known as the Isle of Avalon, and is frequently mentioned in the tales of King Arthur's court.

In the closing years of the twelfth century King

Henry II instituted a search for the burial place of the legendary King Arthur. Giraldus Cambrensis writes that Henry's men found a deeply-buried oak coffin containing the bones of a huge man who had evidently died of head wounds and at his feet the skeleton of a long-haired blonde woman. Atop the coffin there was a heavy leaden cross which identified the occupants of the tomb as King Arthur and his second wife, Guinevere.

The death of Arthur marked the peak of Glastonbury's importance. It had already fallen upon lean days when Henry VIII's grasping hand squeezed the last drop out of it, hanging its last abbot on the hill beside the Abbey. The buildings were blasted apart with gunpowder, the stones were ground up and burnt for lime, the libraries scattered over the countryside by illiterate plunderers. After a thousand years, at least, the massive structure was crumbled by vandals who had been its neighbors.

That was the situation in 1907 when the British archeologist and architect, Frederick Bligh-Bond, undertook the task of excavating the ruins to determine the true extent of the structure. Among other things, he sought the location and size of two chapels, one dedicated to Edgar, the Martyr King, and the other known as the Chapel of Our Lady of Loretto. The structures had been mentioned in early descriptions of the Abbey, but where they were located and what they were like, nobody knew. It was a good starting point for the excavators but an exceedingly vague one.

In his subsequent description of what happened, Bligh-Bond recounts that he was in his office in Bristol on November 7, 1907, with a close personal friend, a Captain Bartlett, who professed to be able to produce messages through what is known as "automatic writing." This is a procedure whereby certain persons produce written messages while consciously engaged otherwise.

Bligh-Bond was aware of Captain Bartlett's activities in this little-understood field as they sat there in his office that day. Purely as an experiment, he asked his friend to take up a pencil. Placing his own fingers lightly on the pencil, Bligh-Bond said: "Can you tell us anything about Glastonbury?"

While he and Bartlett discussed some hunting experiences they had shared in years gone by, the pencil scrawled a single wavy line: "All knowledge is eternal and is available to mental sympathy."

To say that the two men were surprised and puzzled by this would be an understatement. They admitted later that they did not know whether to regard this as a beginning or an end: Were they being told to go dig up the answers for themselves—or to ask and be told? They decided to ask.

On that same day, in response to questions from Bligh-Bond, the automatic writing told the two men, this time in the debased Latin of centuries long gone by, that the Chapel of Edgar the Martyr was first constructed by Abbot Beere and later revised by Abbot Whiting, the last master of Glastonbury. Then Bartlett's hand slowly scrawled out an outline map of the Abbey at its peak, including a peculiar extension of the form which Bligh-Bond suspected was one of his goals. Was it a chapel, he asked?

Tediously the pencil in Bartlett's hand spelled out the answer: "—an entrance back of the reredos, back of the altar, five feet, and the chapel extended thirty yards to the east and windows with horizontal stones called transoms —windows with blue glass."

Yes, the entity calling itself Gulielmus Monachus (William the Monk) was saying that this was Edgar's Chapel, long since destroyed and lost.

Was this true?

Using the measurements and location given in this strange fashion, Bligh-Bond's workmen soon uncovered the ruins of a structure that had extended ninety feet to the east. The location checked with that of the automatic writing but was this really the Chapel of Edgar, which the writing had said was built with a fan vaulted ceiling? Further excavations and a study of the stones disclosed the mason's marks which settled the question. They showed not only the fan-vaulted ceiling but the *type* of fan vaulting that had been used. And the blue glass fragments from the windows were scattered over the stones, just as the vandals had left them.

And what of the other missing chapel? Again Bligh-Bond and Bartlett resorted to the enchanted pencil and again it responded, but this time it wrote in the English of the early 16th Century. When the instructions called for digging in the difficult hard bank of earth on the north side of the Abbey, the excavators decided to re-check their source and were told: "Seek ye my chapel, as I told ye, in ye Banke." It added that only one wall would be found, the rest had been carried away by looters for private construction. The digging confirmed the accuracy of this strange information once again.

Over a period of ten years, Bligh-Bond and Bartlett accumulated hundreds of such messages, all through the so-called automatic writing process. They carefully dated and filed the material and were astounded at the accuracy of the measurements given, some of which proved to be correct within a fraction of an inch after the subjects were uncovered.

In the ten-year course of these curious transactions Bligh-Bond and his friend sought some identification for their communicants. The pencil wrote that these were the monks who had lived at Glastonbury during its entire existence; that each of them was replying to the questions covering the periods with which they, as individuals, were conversant. The occasional long pauses, the pencil wrote, were the result of conferences when the question proved troublesome or when there was some doubt as to just how best to answer it.

One of the most voluminous communicants signed himself Johannes Bryant and claimed to have been a roly-poly fellow who had died in 1533. One of the earliest signatures that appeared on Bartlett's pad was that of a character who scribbled slowly "Awfwold ye Saxon" who claimed that long before the Abbey itself was built on that particular part of the hill, he had constructed a stout wattle-work hut at a spot later covered by the Abbey. Bligh-Bond and his crew excavated at the place which had been carefully identified in the statement and found the easily-identifiable remains of wattlework which had been there when the stones were laid, at least a thousand years before.

Authorities were jubilant at Bligh-Bond's success in locating the long lost portions of the Abbey, including some segments whose existence had not even been suspected. But when they learned that he was basing his search on messages obtained through "automatic writing," they

125

threw up their hands in horror. It was quite all right for him to make the discoveries but he would have to stick to conventional methods!

In 1922 they ruled him off the course, although they had already accepted his findings and extolled its virtues. But they were not done with him yet, nor with his works.

In 1933, Frederick Bligh-Bond wrote a book, *The Gate of Remembrance,* in which he noted not only the messages which he had verified by excavation, but descriptions of other portions of the great Abbey still to be found. Subsequent digging by officially-approved groups merely served to confirm the messages which Bligh-Bond had published years before.

24

Who Was Patience Worth?

Whether Patience Worth ever was a living human being no man can say, but the irrefutable evidence of her wit and wisdom is available in many libraries today in the form of the five books she wrote. If Patience Worth was not a living person then who *did* write the books?

That is a question which scientists who investigated the case were never able to answer. And in view of the complexity of the circumstances and of their variance with accepted scientific concepts, the investigators may be pardoned.

One night in June of 1913, Mr. and Mrs. John H. Curran of St. Louis were entertaining some friends in their home. They were having fun with an Ouija board, which skittered from letter to letter as it seemed to be spelling out answers to their questions.

This parlor pastime had gone on for an hour and a half and had begun to pall on those who were manipulating the board. Mrs. Curran and one of the other ladies present paused for several minutes, their hands still on the device, while they waited for someone to dream up another question to be answered.

Suddenly the planchette came to life. Nobody had asked a question and neither of the ladies at the table were consciously seeking any reply. But the Ouija moved on, spelling out, letter by letter:

"Many moons ago I lived; again I come—Patience Worth is my name."

The puzzled and startled little gathering burst into laughter. Surely one of the ladies at the table was playing a trick?

Mrs. Curran and her friend were as confused as the others. Everyone gathered around the table.

"Patience, where was your home?" asked Mrs. Curran.

There was a pause of perhaps a full minute, then the Ouija began to move in reply.

"Across the sea."

"In what country across the sea?"

Another long pause.

"About me you would know much. Yesterday is dead. Let thy mind rest as to the past."

Then as suddenly as "Patience" had manifested herself she dropped out of the activity. Those present were bewildered by the experience, and skeptical, too, for there was no explanation for it unless it was a harmless little trick being played by Mrs. Curran or the other lady, both of whom disclaimed any such prank.

In the ensuing months, Mrs. Curran discovered that she had only to sit down at the Ouija board and rest her hands on the planchette and messages from "Patience" would come streaming in. Others tried it with the same device but only Mrs. Curran got results.

Soon the cumbersome Ouija board sessions gave way to what is called "automatic writing"—a procedure in which Mrs. Curran sat down with pencil in hand, completely relaxed both mentally and physically, and suddenly the pencil would begin pouring out a torrent of words— thoughts couched in the quaint vernacular of the seventeenth century. There came poetry, quips and axioms galore, some of them unquestionably the work of a brilliant mind.

To suggest that this was the work of Mrs. Curran's own subconscious mind would have been flying in the face of the facts. She could best be described as the typical housewife of her time; a former farm girl with a high school education, pleasant, sincere and likable. Her school records showed that she had little interest or receptivity for either history or composition. The few assignments that she had written were barely passable.

All of this served to rule out the possibility that, through the mythical personality of "Patience Worth," Mrs. Curran was simply releasing a pent-up desire to express herself. Careful investigation by eminent authorities showed that Mrs. Curran had no such desire and no such ability.

By the time Patience Worth had been asserting herself for a year, Mrs. Curran had reached a point where she could manifest this other personality by simply relaxing in a chair, closing her eyes and, as she described it "letting the words come tumbling out, with no thought or effort on my part whatever. I would feel only a pressure on top of my head, as though a hand had been laid on it—and Patience just took over."

As this strange story developed, more and more questions were put to Patience—and little by little the replies shaped into a vague sort of background.

For one thing, it was clear that Patience had been of English origin. She claimed she was born at Dorsetshire in 1650, and brought to New England in 1670. She spoke knowingly and intimately of the rugged existence in the colonies and declared that she had been killed by Indians only a short time after coming to the New World.

One professor, curious as to whether she was referring to King Phillip's War, asked Patience if the name of the Indian who killed her was Phillip.

She snapped back: "If someone had a sword at thy throat, wouldst thee stop to inquire his name?"

It was inevitable that word of such a performance would reach the newspapers and the medical profession. They came and investigated and went away to ponder what they had found. Mrs. Curran cooperated with them to the fullest. She never went into a trance, real or simulated. She simply sat there in her own living room and through her the learned visitors could ask questions of the mysterious Patience and receive prompt, and sometimes pithy, replies.

Patience was cagey. She evaded questions about her present whereabouts and circumstances. She snapped sharp answers to those who tried to misquote some previous statement she had made or to trip her up with sly questions. On one such occasion when she had devastated a visiting professor with a witty retort, he replied that she was certainly clever and Patience promptly came back: "Not so. The stuff was stolen." From whom was it stolen? Patience simply ignored the question.

From her enigmatic statements, the investigators gradually assembled a substantial number of items which were worthy of further checking. For instance, landmarks which Patience mentioned as existing in her seventeenth century youth. Researchers found many of them still extant; others were confirmed by historical and religious records and by old maps. Patience had known her countryside well.

Peculiarities of speech, and words which have no present meaning, were sprinkled through the outpourings of Patience Worth, and led to the suspicion that they were mere figments of the imagination, conjured up to lend color without meaning. But again, when the researchers dug into the musty volumes in the British Museum, Patience was fully sustained by the evidence. Generally the terms she used were colloquialisms of the time in which she claimed to have lived, temporary parts of speech long since forgotten.

In all, Patience Worth is credited with the authorship of five books dictated through Mrs. Curran, generally at the rate of about one hundred and ten words per minute. It is worth noting in this instance that the dictation was made without any interruption for the inevitable corrections and other changes necessitated by the development of a story. Patience simply began and drove steadily forward to the end of the production. The dictations were not continuous, of course; for upon occasion Mrs. Curran would have to forego the transmission for days. But, when she was ready again, Patience began exactly where she had left off.

One of the books she dictated was *The Sorry Tale*, a splendidly-executed novel of the time and life of Christ. Although Mrs. Curran herself had only a casual acquaintance with the subject, the book is noteworthy for the

131

wealth of detail concerning the period in which it deals. W. T. Allison, professor of English literature at the University of Manitoba said of it: "No book outside the Bible gives such an intimate picture of the earthly life of Jews and Romans in Palestine in the days of our Lord."

There were other books from the same source: *The Pot upon the Wheel, Hope True-Blood* and *The Light from Beyond,* as well as a book of poems. Using only the Anglo-Saxon language of 1650, Patience dictated a seventy-thousand-word poem in thirty-five hours. She explained that she was going to perform this feat to prove that she was an independent personality and not a part of Mrs. Curran's mind, subconscious or otherwise.

The resultant poem, called *Telka,* would be a difficult production for a scholar who had spent a lifetime specializing in seventeenth-century speech. The poem itself is slow reading for anyone not familiar with the Anglo-Saxon usage of three hundred years ago. Professor F. S. Schiller of Oxford examined *Telka* and declared that its vocabulary was ninety percent pure Anglo-Saxon. He found the word "amuck" to be the only exception, and even that made its appearance in the English language about 1650, the year in which Patience claimed to have been born. Of the poem and its construction, Professor Schiller said: "We are face to face with a philological miracle."

Newspapers and magazines devoted a great deal of space to the strange experience of Mrs. Curran. Some of them tried to do an honest job of reporting what they found, even though they did not understand its nature. Others, seeking expanded circulation rather than factual reporting, went to considerable length to imply fraud. Unable to specify just what fraud they were hinting at, they quoted mythical observers and the speculations of minor local figures who ofttimes did not even know the circumstances and conditions under which the dictation was performed.

During a period of about fifteen years, Mrs. Curran was visited by no fewer than thirty-five eminent scientists and investigated by them to the extent and in the manner they requested. Not all of them were willing to subscribe to the belief that Patience Worth was what she claimed to be, a personality of centuries gone by, but not one of the investigators who actually investigated ever accused Mrs. Curran of fraud, voluntary or otherwise.

A fine example of the oblique escape used by some of the extremely cautious scholars is that presented by Professor G. H. Estabrook of Colgate, who was unwilling to subscribe to the theory that Mrs. Curran was actually voicing the words and thoughts of a personality long dead. However, Professor Estabrook did venture the opinion that the case was very complex ". . . showing to a very high degree that ingenuity of the unconscious so evident in hypnotism."

His statement, to paraphrase his own words, shows to a very high degree the ingenuity of scientists who are faced with something they can't explain. Mrs. Curran was never "unconscious" and there was absolutely no "hypnotism" involved.

There are many unexplainable facets to the incredible case of Patience Worth. Her sharp tongue, keen to the point of impertinence, was in marked contrast to the personality of Mrs. Curran. Once, when asked to explain precisely where she was located, Patience snapped: "A hen betrays not its nest by a loud cackle!" And where did she get the ideas for her books? asked another investigator.

Patience promptly replied: "To brew a potion, one needs must have a pot!"

A group of visiting psychologists asked Patience to perform a feat that they considered impossible: She was asked to dictate about three hundred words on a book then in progress, to be followed by a few minutes' conversation, then three hundred words on another book, followed by more conversation . . . all dictations to be ended at the will of the doctor who made the request. Patience agreed and the test began.

Suddenly the doctor cried: "Stop! Now give us a poem —on dust!"

Without hesitation, Patience responded by dictating:
"Dust, dust, dust,—the mould of kings,
  Bit of the Orient, ashes of wise men,
  The clod from the foot of the fool,
  Dead roses, withered leaves, crumbling
  Palaces, men's hopes and desires,
  The tears of ages, and stuff of all mankind.
  Dust, dust, awaiting the hand of God
  To intermingle and resurrect.
  Dust, dust, dust—tomorrow unborn
  Dust, dust, yesterday's ashes."

Then Patience, on order, resumed dictating the book. The doctor suddenly called for some proverbs, which were instantly forthcoming and including such examples as:
"When manna falls, fill thyself and question not."
"Loud noises from the mouth are born in an empty head."
"Weak yarn is not worth the knitting."

Having fulfilled this assignment without hesitation, Patience paused for instruction. The doctor asked her to

134

dictate two more poems on topics he specified and again the poems came tumbling from the lips of Mrs. Curran while a couple of secretaries recorded what was said.

It was a feat virtually impossible for any human being and it was small wonder that the group of specialists who witnessed the performance admitted they were baffled. Yet, remarkable as it was, it was but a small part of the even greater and equally mystifying record of the manifestation of Patience Worth; a riddle to which the books she wrote exist to this day as question marks for which science has yet found no acceptable answer.

25

Jacques Cazotte: Prophet With Honor

The great trouble with many prophecies is that they may well have been made *after* the event, and many of them undoubtedly were. But that was not the case with the predictions made by Jacques Cazotte, a meek, mild-mannered poet of modest renown who was present at a garden party given by the Duchess de Gramont on a summer evening in France, 1788. Fortunately for the records, Cazotte's words were taken down by a skeptic who planned to use them to ridicule their source.

The poet was a familiar figure to the brilliant assemblage at that particular party, for he had been a protégé of the hostess for many years and had often read his works to her guests. In the vernacular of our times he would have been regarded as an "odd ball," for Cazotte chose to be alone in the midst of the crowd, a self-appointed isolationist who remained aloof on a bench by the fountain, by turns dreaming or mumbling to himself; an island of solemnity in a sea of gaiety.

But the spark that touched him off was a toast given by

Guillaume des Malesherbes, Minister and confidant to Louis XIV, who said:

"A toast to the day when reason will be triumphant in the affairs of men—although I shall never live to see the day!"

As the ripple of laughter died down and the glasses were raised, Cazotte slowly rose from his bench and limped forward to confront the Minister. Leaning his gnarled little hands heavily on his cane, Cazotte said hoarsely:

"You are wrong, sir! You *will* live to see the day—for it shall come within six years!"

The throng was silent.

Was this glassy-eyed old man insane, or was this his idea of a joke?

Turning to the Marquis de Condorcet, Cazotte said, "You will cheat the executioner by taking poison!"

This brought a thin ripple of uneasy giggles from the crowd and, before it had subsided, Cazotte had turned to still another of the dignitaries, Chamfort, the King's favorite.

"You, Chamfort, will slash your wrist twenty-two times with your razor, but it will not kill you. You will live a long life thereafter."

"And, you, Monsieur Bailly," he said to the famous astronomer, "in spite of your good deeds and great learning there lies ahead only death by execution at the hands of the mob."

Minister des Malesherbes sought to turn Cazotte's grim predictions off as a jest by bowing low before the little poet.

"Pray tell us, sire," he said, "since you seem to know so much about so many of my ill-fated friends, can you also end my breathless concern about my own fate?"

137

Cazotte placed a hand on the Minister's shoulder and looked him straight in the face.

"I regret to inform you, sir, that your fate shall be the counterpart of that which awaits your friend Chamfort. You, too, shall die as a public spectacle in the executioner's dock."

By this time the shock was wearing off and natural gaiety was reasserting itself. To deliver the *coup de grace* to this nonsensical performance, the fanatical atheist, Jean La Harpe, stepped forward. He despised Cazotte and the feeling was mutual.

"And what of me, sir? You do me ill by neglecting my neck while you send all my friends to the executioner! I beg to be permitted to join them that we may hiss at the mob together! Surely you can grant me this last favor?"

The crowd roared at this bit of satire, but Cazotte remained stony-faced and unmoved.

"I should like nothing better—but the Fates deny me, too. Monsieur La Harpe, they have saved a more fitting destiny for you. You will escape the executioner's axe—only to become a devout Christian!"

Duchess de Gramont waited until the gales of laughter had subsided before she said to Cazotte, with a simulated pout, that the executioners seemed to be sparing the ladies.

He gazed sadly at her for a moment and then took both her hands in his. "Alas, my good friend, the executioners have poor regard for the finest of ladies. It is a day when it will be fatal to be noble, even for the ladies. You will die like the King himself, after riding to the scaffold in a wood cutter's cart!"

The King executed? Preposterous!

Five years after Jacques Cazotte made his prophecy it

was confirmed in every detail by the French Revolution. And the prophecy itself was set down on the night it was uttered in the diary of the atheist Jean La Harpe, who wanted to use it to humiliate Cazotte when the time limit had expired. When La Harpe died, he willed the document to the monastery where he had found his faith, just as Cazotte had predicted.

26

He Sees Through
The Earth

One of the strangest talents on record is that of a Canadian businessman who has confused scientists with his apparent ability to see deep into solid earth.

J. Raoul Derosiers frequently suffered from sharp stabbing pains under the lower ribs on both sides of his body. The attacks were generally painful but of short duration and he paid little attention to them. However, in 1940 the seizures came more frequently and lasted so much longer that Mr. Derosiers went to the doctor. That gentleman listened patiently, decided it was largely if not entirely psychological, and prescribed some sleeping pills. A good night's rest, perhaps—a refreshed mind—presto! No pain!

That was the theory and it seemed to work, for a time at least.

After he had been taking the pills for about a month, Derosiers went to visit the farm of a relative in Quebec. The relative complained that he was being forced out of the cattle business by lack of water. Derosiers sympathized but beyond that had nothing to contribute. Then, a few moments later, as the two men were walking across a field behind the barns, he got one of those terrible pains in his ribs. Turning to his cousin he said: "Don't ask me why I say this, for I can't explain it—but I feel that I am standing over a stream of underground water . . . good water. It is seventy feet down and it runs over the top of a layer of slate three inches thick. Don't drill through that slate or you will lose the water!"

Three weeks later the well was drilled at the spot Derosiers had indicated and an ample supply of potable water was hit just one foot deeper than he had indicated. It bottomed out on a layer of slate, too, but the driller carefully refrained from punching through that. Later drilling a short distance away indicated that the slate ranged from three to four inches in thickness.

Word of this "water witching" got around quickly and Derosiers found his services much in demand. He selected sites for more than six hundred wells without failure, simply by stopping when he got that stabbing pain in his ribs.

Canadian government officials and men of science from several institutions have put him to every test they can think of. Some sought to expose him as a fraud, others tried to determine how he does it. They found that the electrical potential of his skin differs from the ordinary man's, but beyond that they could detect no significant change or variation.

Somehow, Raoul Derosiers has developed an uncanny ability to describe in detail the layers of rock and slate and sand over which he happens to be standing when the pain strikes him in the ribs. Whether the sleeping pills brought about some change in him which made this possible is a matter of conjecture. At any rate, he is one of the strange people of our time—with an ability he never had before and has had ever since. According to his clients, Derosiers never misses.

27

Child Prophet

The little eight-year-old girl who stood in the midst of a throng of French nobility was the daughter of a servant in the home of the Duc d'Orleans' mistress. The child was timid, illiterate and frightened. In her hand she held a glass of water which the Duc had just placed there.

Was it true that this youngster could sometimes foretell the future by gazing into a glass of water and describing what she saw there? Rumor among the servants said that she had predicted some surprising events well in advance by such a simple process, so the Duc had sent for her.

"Tell me, my child, is it true that you can see the future in this glass of water, as so many have claimed for you? If it be true, how will the scene appear when King Louis dies? What do you see in his bedchamber at that moment? Can you tell me?"

Staring fixedly into the glass of water, the little girl began to speak. A hush fell over those in the room, for this little girl was describing in detail a room she had never seen, the bedchamber of King Louis XIV. She described

face after face of those present and the clothing each wore
. . . and where they stood in the room.

When she had finished the Duc was puzzled.

"You see no other faces? Not even these?" He pointed
to several persons who were present at the moment, including the Duc and Duchess of Bourgogne and the Duc de Beri.

The child again gazed into the water and shook her
head slowly. "No," she whispered, "I do not see them for
they are not there."

Eight years later, at the death of Louis XIV, the scene
was precisely as the little girl had described it to the Duc
d'Orleans, a matter which was easy to check because several
copies of her prediction had been taken down by interested
parties. And those whom she could not see on that memorable afternoon were not present. They had all died before
the King.

28

Shanti Devi —
A Living Riddle

If she had not lived before, the investigators could offer no reasonable solution to her incredible case. If she had lived before then she was all the more incredible. But whatever the answer might be, there are no cases more strange than hers and none better documented by the eminent men who investigated.

It is a matter of record that Shanti Devi was born in Delhi, India, in 1926. Her parents were well-to-do though not wealthy. There was nothing unusual about her birth—nothing to warn either parents or doctor of what was to come.

When Shanti was about three years old her parents noticed that she persistently spoke of her husband and of her children. At first they passed this off as nothing more than the imaginative prattle of a playful and rather lonely child, but when she persisted the parents become concerned.

Who was this "husband"? Where did he live?

The child calmly assured her mother that the "husband" was named Kedarnath and she and he had lived in a city

145

called Muttra. She described in detail the house where they had lived, and claimed that she had had a son who still lived there with his father.

By this time, thoroughly alarmed lest the child be losing her mind, the parents took her to the family physician. He had already heard the unusual version from her parents and he expected the child to recant or at least to refuse to repeat it to him. The doctor did not know his patient, for little Shanti sat there in the big chair in his office, hands folded in her lap, and repeated to him everything she had told her parents and more. Among other things she said that she had died in childbirth in 1925, about one year before she was born in Delhi. The bewildered doctor questioned her closely about the aspects of her alleged pregnancy and the child astounded him by giving details which merely compounded the mystery. She unquestionably was describing the physical and mental aspects of a troublesome pregnancy which, young as she was, she could not have undergone.

By the time she was seven she had been questioned by half a dozen doctors and she left all of them completely puzzled. At the age of eight her grand-uncle, Professor Kishen Chand, decided that it was high time someone did more than merely talk to the child. Was there a fellow named Kedarnath in Muttra? Did he have a son and had he lost his wife named Ludgi in childbirth in 1925? Those questions, and others pertinent to the case, the Professor put into a letter which he mailed to this mysterious "Kedarnath" in Muttra at the address so frequently mentioned by Shanti in Delhi.

There *was* such a man and he got the letter. At first he suspected a trap of some sort, perhaps an attempt to defraud him of his property, so he declined to meet this girl who claimed to have been his wife until he checked on the matter—for which one can hardly blame him. Accordingly, Kedarnath of Muttra wrote to a cousin in Delhi, a man who had often visited at Kedarnath's home while Ludgi was living. He would certainly recognize her if he saw her—and after all, Ludgi was the only wife Kedarnath had ever had. Would the cousin please make an excuse to visit the address where this person lived, to see for himself what this was all about?

The cousin made a pretext of conducting business with Shanti's father and arranged to call at the Devi's home.

The child, now nine years old, was helping her mother prepare the evening meal when there was a knock at the door. The little girl ran to open it. Puzzled when the child did not return after a reasonable length of time the mother went to see for herself. There stood Shanti, staring in apparent amazement at the equally amazed gentleman who waited outside the door.

"Mother! This is the cousin of my husband! He, too, lived in Muttra—not far from where we lived!"

A moment later Shanti's father arrived and the cousin told his story. He did not recognize the child, of course, although she had certainly recognized *him*. He told the child's parents that he had a cousin named Kedarnath who lived in Muttra and that the cousin's wife, Ludgi, had indeed died in childbirth about one year before Shanti Devi's birth. The couple had a small son of whom Ludgi had been very fond at the time of her death.

What to do next? The grand-uncle who had written the letter which resulted in the visit from Kedarnath's cousin was called. It was decided that Shanti's parents should invite Kedarnath to visit them with his son, at their expense and without Shanti's knowledge of their plan.

A few days later Kedarnath arrived. Shanti let out a cry of joy and ran to the child, who was understandably taken aback by this attention from a person he had never seen before. Shanti tried to pick him up, but he was as large as she was. She hugged him and called him the same pet names that Ludgi had used before she died ten years previously. And to Kedarnath, Shanti conducted herself in the manner of an overjoyed but dutiful wife, just as Ludgi had done.

It was a weird experience for all who were present.

Kedarnath declined to leave his son with this excited child who claimed to be the boy's mother; instead, he made a hasty exit and returned to Muttra to think about this baffling and rather frightening affair in which he found himself an unwilling participant.

Reports of the incident got into the newspapers and created widespread interest. Was it a hoax? How did this child in Delhi know the intimate details of a family in Muttra—a family she had never seen and of whom her own parents had no knowledge whatever?

Desh Bandu Gupta, president of the All-India Newspaper Publishers Association and also a member of the Indian Parliament, conferred with some of his colleagues both in government and in the publishing business. They came to the conclusion that here was a case that merited full and careful investigation. They decided that the acid test would be to take the child to Muttra, to see if she could guide them to the house in which she claimed to have lived and died.

Accompanied by Shanti's parents, Mr. Gupta, an advocate named Tara C. Mathur and other eminent scholars and citizens boarded the train for Muttra.

The surprises began when the train arrived at the station in Muttra. Without hesitation Shanti identified the mother and brother of her alleged husband; furthermore she conversed with them in the colloquial dialect of the area and not in the Hindustani which she had been taught at home in Delhi.

Could she find her way in a town she had never seen to a house where she claimed to have lived as the wife of Kedarnath? She would try. The party got into a couple of carriages that had been provided and started off through the winding streets, carrying out the instructions of the girl. Once or twice she seemed confused, but given time to think it over, she chose the correct route and unerringly led the party to the house which she claimed to recognize.

"Here it is!" she said to the investigators. "This is the house—but in my days it was painted yellow. Now it is white."

There had been still another change since 1925. Kedarnath had moved from that house and the people who now lived there refused to admit the girl and the crowd that milled around her.

Shanti asked to be taken to the present residence of her "husband." When the party arrived there she immediately recognized the two oldest children of Kedarnath but did not recognize the ten year old whose birth had cost Ludgi's life. Taken next to the home of Ludgi's mother, Shanti recognized the aged woman at once and ran to her crying "Mother! Mother!" The woman was startled and confused at this outburst—for although this child talked like Ludgi and acted like Ludgi and remem-

149

bered the things Ludgi would have remembered—the old lady knew that her Ludgi had been dead all these years.

At the home of Ludgi's mother, Mr. Gupta asked Shanti if she noticed any changes that had been made in the place since she claimed to have last seen it. Without hesitation the child pointed to a spot where she said a well was missing. Sure enough, a well which had been located there had been covered over with heavy planks years before and was buried from sight.

Kedarnath asked Shanti if she remembered what Ludgi had done with the rings she had concealed shortly before her death and which he had never been able to find. Shanti told him they were buried in an earthen pot under a board in a corner of the garden behind his former home. He found them there, along with a few small coins, just as Shanti had said.

All the attendant publicity became most unwelcome to Shanti and to the family of Kedarnath in Muttra. The children did not know her and did not want to know her. Kedarnath's attitude was one of tolerant confusion. Shanti Devi retreated into comparative seclusion to avoid being stared at and pointed out wherever she went. Little by little she fought down the desire to be with Kedarnath and the children. Little by little, after a long and torturous mental struggle, she managed to force herself to create an existence which did not interfere with theirs.

Professor Indra Sen, of Sri Aurobindo's Ashram at Pondicherry, has the full documentation on Shanti Devi's astounding case history. The scientists who took part in the probe and who evaluated the evidence were guarded in their summations. They agreed that somehow a child born in Delhi in 1926 seemed to remember in great clarity and detail a life in Muttra. They reported that they could find no evidence of trickery and no explanation for what they had seen.

And what of Shanti Devi? In 1958 the *Washington Post* and other papers around the world carried the account of an interview with her. They found her living quietly as a government clerk in New Delhi; a rather shy, quiet and resigned young woman of thirty-two.

She had learned to live in the present, she told reporters and medical interrogators; the old yearning to return to the past had been subdued after a long hard struggle and she does not care to revive it.

29

The Incredible Case Of Lurancy Vennum

Could a girl suddenly acquire the memories and mannerisms of a person whom she had never known or seen—a person who had been dead for twelve years?

Investigators (and there were many of them) never found an answer that they cared or dared to make public. Perhaps their trepidation was justified, for the case of Lurancy Vennum was one where an acceptance of the obvious constituted admission of the unthinkable.

In order to examine the story of Lurancy Vennum we must first set down the facts about her predecessor, Mary Roff, with whom her name became inextricably entwined. Mary was the daughter of Mr. and Mrs. Asa Roff and she was born in Warren County, Indiana, October 8, 1846. When she was thirteen years old her parents moved the family to Watseka, Illinois.

By that time Mary's health had been undermined by seizures which were probably epileptic. She suffered these attacks at the rate of two a day in the spring of 1865 and to escape from her misery she tried suicide by slashing her wrists. The family found her unconscious from loss of blood and summoned a doctor. When Mary recovered consciousness she became so violent that for several hours it required the combined efforts of several adults to hold her in bed—a surprising show of strength for a hundred pound girl in her condition.

After five days of this raving she suddenly became calm and dropped off in a sleep that lasted more than fifteen hours. Upon awakening, she made no attempt to remove the bandages which had been placed over her eyes to protect them from her unconscious clawing; instead, she seemed to be able to see as readily while blindfolded as she had before.

Friends of the family, including A. J. Smith, editor of the *Danville Times,* and the Reverend J. H. Rhea, were present when Mary Roff, heavily blindfolded, correctly "read" to them the contents of an unopened letter in the editor's pocket and sorted without error a stack of old letters which she could not see by any known procedure. The startled editor wrote a lengthy and detailed account of this occurrence in his paper.

Gradually, the young girl's condition deteriorated to such an extent that doctors advised her parents to commit her to a mental institution immediately. They refused. Instead, the parents took turns caring for Mary and when they visited friends in Peoria for the Fourth of July holiday in 1865, Mary was with them. The following morning she complained of a terrible headache and left the breakfast table. A few moments later they found her dead in her bed. The coroner's report listed brain convulsions as the cause of death.

On the day that Mary Roff died, Lurancy Vennum was

a fifteen-month-old baby living on her parents' farm in Iowa. The family of Thomas Vennum moved to a farm seven miles south of Watseka, Illinois, in 1871, almost six years after the death of Mary Roff; so it is certain that Lurancy Vennum never saw Mary.

Lurancy was thirteen years old and considered a normal, healthy child when the twelfth anniversary of Mary Roff's death rolled around on July 5, 1877. She surprised her parents the next morning by saying, "There were people in my room last night and they kept calling 'Rancy! Rancy!' and I could feel their breath on my face."

On the following night the child underwent the same experience, but it ended when her mother spent the rest of the night with Lurancy.

It was just one week after she first complained of the "People" in her room that Lurancy Vennum's real troubles began. She was helping her mother stitch a broken seam in a carpet when she straightened and exclaimed, "Maw, I feel bad; I feel mighty queer!" A moment later she stiffened into a trance-like condition which lasted for five hours.

These trances became daily occurrences until September of 1877 and usually consisted of Lurancy lying in a rigid state, her pulse weak, her breath slow and faint, her temperature below normal. She would mutter weakly of strange sights which ofttimes included descriptions of what she called angels.

Dotors who examined her were unable to agree whether she was mentally unbalanced, temporarily deranged by epileptic seizures or suffering from some rare disease which they could not identify. But the references to "angels" tipped the scales in favor of a general verdict of mental instability. Whatever the cause, the doctors were unable

154

to alleviate the condition. By November, Lurancy was suffering from such excruciating abdominal pains that she would bend backward until her feet touched her head, often entering her trance-like state while in this position.

January, 1878, found the child's parents exhausted and at their wit's end. Lurancy was having trances at the rate of ten to twelve a day. Some of them lasted only a few minutes, others lasted for hours. She would go into these spells at all hours of the day and night and generally mumble descriptions of "bright angels" and seemed to hold conversations with invisible beings.

The distraught parents finally called upon the Reverend B. M. Baker, pastor of the Watseka Methodist Church, for any help he could give. The minister had listened to several of Lurancy's "conversations" with invisible beings and decided that the child was mad. He promptly took it upon himself to contact an insane asylum to see if they would accept the girl as a patient.

The story of Lurancy Vennum's strange trances and of her alleged conversations with "angels" spread rapidly through the community and, when Mr. and Mrs. Roff heard of them, they were reminded of some of the experiences they had had with their own daughter, Mary, many years before. She, too, had suffered from seizures and trances and had muttered of the strange bright beings with whom she seemed to be conversing. Was Lurancy Vennum traveling the same path?

At the suggestion of the Roffs, Mr. and Mrs. Vennum postponed sending Lurancy to a mental institution. Instead they took the Roff's advice and called in a Dr. E. W. Stevens of Janesville, Wisconsin. He arrived on January 31, 1878, to find Lurancy seated in a small rocking chair beside the stove, staring dully at the floor. As Dr. Stevens approached, she twisted the chair around to face him and warned him to keep his distance.

He sat down and talked with the family and with Mr. Roff, his personal friend, who was also present. They discussed matters which had no connection with the girl for half an hour, until Dr. Stevens turned to her and said: "I don't believe I have met you, young lady. What is your name?"

"Katrina Hogan!" Lurancy snapped.

Further questioning brought out that "Katrina Hogan" was sixty-three and had come from Germany three days before, *"by air."* How long would she stay? Three weeks.

Patiently, bit by bit, Dr. Stevens led the girl through an hour of this type of give-and-take. Lurancy appeared to gain confidence in him, and the others who were present remained discreetly silent. Suddenly she rose from her chair and fell forward, stiff as a board. Dr. Stevens caught her and laid her gently on the floor. Lurancy's lips began to move but they made no intelligible sounds for perhaps ten minutes. Then they heard her telling Katrina Hogan to go away and she ordered others to get out too. They were all characters whose names were meaningless to those present at the Vennum home.

As she lapsed into a period of silence, Dr. Stevens asked the girl if she would not prefer to be controlled by better people. Lurancy replied, "Yes. There are many spirits here who would be glad to come."

And after a moment's silence she added:

"One of them is Mary Roff!"

The startled father of the dead girl exclaimed:

"Mary! That's my daughter! She has been dead for

years. . . . Yes, let her come! We'll be glad to have her come!"

Lurancy then appeared to be holding a conversation with "Mary," and finally she said that Mary Roff would come and "take the place of" the characters such as the Katrina Hogan whom she had previously mentioned. Then Lurancy smiled and relaxed and the session was ended.

The Vennums got the shock of their lives next morning when Lurancy, the violent, unpredictable girl who had to be watched every moment, became congenial, polite and docile. Nor was that all—for Lurancy Vennum apparently recognized none of her family. Instead, she contended she was Mary Roff—and wanted to go home!

The befuddled Thomas Vennum rushed over to the Roff home several blocks away and appraised them of this latest development. Lurancy, said her father, was acting like a homesick youngster who kept repeating that she wanted to see her Ma and Pa and the rest of the family.

The Roffs were nonplused; they had not anticipated such a surprising contretemps. After a hasty consultation with Mr. Vennum, it was decided that they would take no action at all for a few days; perhaps this was only a passing fancy that would go away if left alone.

It was not a fancy. Lurancy continued to treat her own family as though they were strangers and to implore them to let her go home. Why were they keeping her from her family whom she had not seen in so many years? Mr. Vennum went back to the Roffs and told them that something had to be done. Would they please come over and let Lurancy see them? It might help—somehow.

Four days after Lurancy startled her family by announcing that she was Mary Roff, Mrs. Roff and her daughter Minerva, the eldest of the family, came to the Vennum home. As they approached on the sidewalk, still half a block from the place, Lurancy glanced up and saw them. She was on her feet in an instant. "It's my mother and my sister Nervie!" she cried. In life, the real Mary Roff had called her eldest sister "Nervie" since she was old enough to pronounce it.

The girl threw herself on Mrs. Roff and Minerva with tears of joy streaming down her face. For them it was a distressing experience. Here was a girl who was not related to them claiming to be the beloved member of their own family whom they knew to be dead. She talked with them about old friends of the Roff family and about the family whom they had been visiting when she died in Peoria thirteen years before. She asked about a little box of letters which Mary Roff had received from friends shortly before her death. Had they saved her letters?

Mr. Roff managed to sob out that she *had* saved them. The girl recounted the messages in some of the letters and, when Mrs. Roff returned to her home that day, she found that the messages were exactly as described.

After the brief visit with Mrs. Roff and Minerva, Lurancy became more insistent that she be taken to live with them. Her parents felt that it would be a burden on the Roffs, for there was a strong probability that this mood would pass and Lurancy would again become a violent mental case, just as the doctors predicted. But the Roffs were convinced by the girl's detailed knowledge of family affairs that this was no mere happenstance. Just what it was they did not know, but there was something altogether remarkable about it.

Lurancy Vennum, as Mary Roff, went to live with the Roffs on February 11, 1878.

It would be a visit that would last only until May, she told them, for the "angels" had granted her only that much time.

Was it really Mary Roff visiting her parents in the person of Lurancy Vennum? If so, where was the real Lurancy?

They put those questions to her and the girl assured them that she was indeed their own daughter, and she would endeavor to prove it. And Lurancy Vennum? She was away, being treated, and would return when she was cured, both mentally and physically. When Lurancy was ready to "come back," Mary would have to leave.

Such a state of affairs was certain to attract wide attention and the inevitable investigation. Dr. Stevens' book *The Watseka Wonder* is a well-written volume based on his personal knowledge of the case. William James also investigated and reported his findings at length. Contemporary newspapers in and around Chicago found the Lurancy Vennum-Mary Roff case a subject of great interest and spent many columns on it.

Standing out from the evidence is the fact that for fifteen weeks Lurancy Vennum lived the life of the departed Mary Roff among Mary's family and friends. Her every mood and mannerism and memory were entirely compatible with those of the real Mary Roff, whom she had never known.

For instance, when Mrs. Roff brought out the box of letters which "Mary" had inquired about, the girl reached into the box and pulled out a little collar. She told Mrs.

Roff it was one she had tatted as a little girl so she could wear it to a party . . . which was true. When Mr. Roff asked her if she could remember when they had moved to Texas (in 1857, when Mary was eleven) the girl promptly replied that she remembered it very well, and especially seeing the Indians along the Red River and of playing with Mrs. Reeder's little girls, who were in the same party of travelers.

She described relatives who had died since the death of Mary Roff and correctly identified pictures and names and relationships of friends of the Roff family. When Mrs. Roff laid out a little velvet skull cap which had belonged to the original Mary, Lurancy promptly picked it up and identified is as the one "she" had worn when her hair was cut short, right after a severe illness. One of the many surprising things she did was to describe in detail the funeral of Mary Roff, including a little incident that had taken place in Mrs. Roff's room shortly before the final services. The only persons present at the incident were the parents of the dead girl and they had never mentioned it to anyone.

Day after day and week after week the weird experience continued. The Roffs were convinced that the girl they knew as Lurancy Vennum had somehow been replaced by their long-dead daughter.

Even Dr. Stevens was surprised when Lurancy turned to him one day in the course of his investigation and asked if he would like news of his daughter, Emma. After he overcame the shock, the doctor replied that he would appreciate such information. Lurancy told him that Emma was happy and that she had recently conversed with her and that Emma wanted her parents to know that she was happy and would like to be with them. The girl went on to describe Emma Angelia Stevens, who had died in March of 1849, and the description was accurate even to an X-shaped scar on the cheek where an infection had required surgery.

However, "Mary Roff's" time was running out.

On April 16, 1878, she told the Roff family that she would soon be leaving them, for Lurancy Vennum was getting well and would return.

On May 7, 1878, "Mary" tearfully called Mrs. Roff to her, took her by the hands and sobbed that she would soon be leaving. They sat thus for several minutes, according to witnesses, and then "Mary" began to shake as if she were having a chill. She slumped forward as though in a faint and remained motionless. A few moments later she opened her eyes in unmistakable bewilderment and gasped, "Where am I?"

Lurancy Vennum was once again Lurancy Vennum.

But only briefly, for "Mary" again took over and continued as before until May 21st. On that day, at 11 a.m., after bidding goodbye to the family and friends and after giving them some advice, "Mary" gave way to Lurancy for the last time.

Since "Mary" had warned the Roffs of the exact time the change would occur, the Vennums were present when Lurancy opened her eyes and came into her own. She told her parents that she felt as though she had been asleep for a long time, although she realized that was not actually the case.

Doctors came and questioned and examined and went away puzzled by what they saw and found. In July of 1878, Dr. Stevens pronounced Lurancy sound as a dollar, both mentally and physically. He received a letter from Lurancy, written in pencil, thanking him for his patience and services. The letter bears no resemblance to other writings which "Mary Roff" had made in the recent past, although the same fingers held the pencil.

Lurancy Vennum became an attractive young woman who married George Binning, a farmer near Watseka. They moved to Rollins County, Kansas, and she became the mother of eleven children. In 1940 she was still alive in California, a seventy-six-year-old woman who preferred not to discuss the fifteen weeks during her girlhood when she baffled science.

The evidence in her case in voluminous. What she did is well attested, but how or why it happened is a matter still to be resolved.

30

The Possession Of
Maria Talarico

The case of Lurancy Vennum happened more than eighty years ago. But there have been strange people with similar histories in our own time.

Under the bridge that spans the Corace River between Siano and Catanzaro, Italy, the body of nineteen-year-old Guiseppe Veraldi was found on the morning of February 13, 1936. It was only partially clothed, most of the garments being scattered about on the river's bank. His head rested on a large stone. The left arm was broken and doubled under his chest.

Police examined the body, ignored the evidence, and decided that "Pepe" Veraldi and his companions of the night before had drunk too much and that on his way home Pepe had brooded over a recent love affair and jumped to his death from the bridge.

Just how ridiculous this assumption was can be ascertained quickly by recognition of the fact that the bridge at that point was more than a hundred feet high. Veraldi suffered only a broken arm and possible concussion. In any case, after having fallen a hundred feet to the stony river bank, he certainly could not have undressed himself; nor would he have escaped with such comparatively minor injuries.

Even an amateur sleuth would have recognized the signs of murder in this case, but the inquest upheld the police verdict and the death of Guiseppe Veraldi was officially closed.

Officially, perhaps, but not closed as far as his friends and relatives were concerned. They knew that he had last been seen alive in the company of four drinking companions—Toto, Damiano, Abele and Rosario. They had been playing cards in a back room at the Gioso Tavern when Veraldi had come in. He took no part in the game but stood with his back to the wall, drinking wine, and kibitzing. Around midnight, witnesses said, the quintet left the tavern and walked toward the bridge where Pepe's body was found the next day.

The police examination of the four men who had been with Veraldi on the night of his death was perfunctory: they were asked where and when they had last seen him and if they had any idea what might have induced him to take his own life. The foursome all agreed they had left him near the bridge and none of them could ascribe any motive for suicide except that he was very drunk.

But the strange story of Pepe Veraldi did not end there, it only began.

Three years after his death on the river bank under the bridge a young girl in Siano, at the other end of that same bridge, suffered from a strange ailment.

Maria Talarico was seventeen, the second of a family of six children. She had not known Veraldi or any of his family and the only time she had ever seen him was when she had gone with other youngsters and peered down from the bridge at his body, more than a hundred feet below, as police conducted their routine inspection of the scene. That had been three years before the strange abnormality struck her.

It began on January 5, 1939, when Maria and her grandmother walked across the bridge to visit Maria's mother, who worked on one of Mussolini's Fascist projects in Catanzaro. Nothing unusual happened until they approached the bridge on the return trip. As they reached the spot nearest the scene of Veraldi's death, Maria suddenly dropped to the ground. There was a terrible pain in her knees, she said. A passerby, Guiseppe Trapasso, came to the aid of the two women and with his help Granny managed to get Maria home and to bed.

Within an hour the girl was clearly out of her mind. She writhed and groaned as though she were in some sort of convulsion. Her voice, normally soft and pleasant, became deep and sharp. She screamed that she wanted to see her mother—*at once!* A neighbor boy ran to the project where Mrs. Talarico worked and she came home as quickly as possible.

Maria took one look at her mother and shook her head.

"You're not my mother!" she screamed. "You may be the owner of this house but you are not my mother. She lives in Catanzaro—on Barrache Street—and her name is Catterina. I am Pepe!"

Questioning brought out that Maria was claiming to be the man whose body had been found under the bridge three years before. She kept calling for her "mother"— Mrs. Catterina Veraldi. Excited villagers soon spread the word that Maria Talarico was insane—that she imagined

165

she was a man long dead—and that her voice and thoughts had changed to those of Pepe Veraldi.

Fortunately for the records on this case, there were competent and methodical medical practitioners in Catanzaro and they entered the case early.

Dr. Giovanni Scambia seems to have been the first medical authority to examine the girl. His office was in Catanzaro and he made a total of fourteen visits to the Talarico home in Siano. Most important, Dr. Scambia kept a complete record of his findings and of the testimony he and the other medics accumulated in connection with the case. Dr. Fragola, a psychiatrist; Dr. Peri, an oculist; Dr. Manzi Carelli, director of the School of Obstetrics at Catanzaro; and Dr. Vincenzo Catalono, also of Catanzaro, all took part in the examination and study of Maria Talarico's strange condition.

In the early stages of her seizure, when "Pepe" kept demanding that his mother be brought to him, Mrs. Talarico told Maria that she would send a note to Mrs. Veraldi. Maria took the pencil and scribbled: "Dear Mother. If you want to see me I am still your poor son. Pepe."

But Mrs. Veraldi never got to see that note, for by this time the Siano police had invited themselves into the strange doings in the modest little Talarico home, and the Chief of Police, Salvatore Malorgio, simply confiscated the note and put it under lock and key.

(Later, Dr. Scambia and the othe medics induced the Chief to let them have the note, which they compared with samples of Guiseppe Veraldi's handwriting and with that of Maria Talarico. They agreed that it was identical to that of Veraldi, although it had been written by Miss Talarico.)

The Possession Of Maria Talarico

On the evening of January 5th, Maria rose from her bed and selected four men from the crowd in the house to play a game of cards. To humor her, they agreed and seated themselves around the table. She gave each of them names, Rosario, Toto, Abele and Damiano—the names of the four men who had been playing cards the night of Veraldi's death. As they played cards, Maria leaned against the wall and smoked cigarettes and drank wine, things which she had never done in her normal state.

As the game progressed, she chided the characters around the little table.

"Why don't you put sugar and salt and poppy seeds in the wine you give me, as you did that night. What do you you want to get me drunk for—so you can kill me?" It was the voice of a man and it was a taunting voice, that of someone certain of the facts.

During the course of the game, Maria drank more than two quarts of wine and presently she became ill and regurgitated. A few moments later she began to scream and thresh about as though trying to defend herself.

"Abelo! Toto! Let me alone. Don't hit me—don't hit me! Help . . . help! . . . They're trying to kill me under the bridge!"

After this outburst she sank down in a stupor for a few minutes and then, as Maria Talarico, spent a sleepless night.

The Veraldis heard of the strange case but they were undecided on whether to become involved. They finally decided to put the girl to a test, so they selected a photograph of a sister of Veraldi whom Maria had certainly never seen. Carito Giovanni, Pepe's brother-in-law, brought the picture to Maria's bedside while she was claiming to be Pepe.

167

The moment the picture was unwrapped Maria grabbed it and called the girl by name. She even recounted a little family incident in which Pepe and the sister had been involved years before and of which the brother-in-law had never heard.

On the following day, according to Dr. Scambia's record, Maria awakened very early. She urged her family to get their house in order, for her "mother," Mrs. Veraldi, would be there at seven o'clock. And as the hour approached she continued to describe Mrs. Veraldi's approach. At precisely 7 a.m. the visitor arrived.

It was a fantastic scene, of course. Maria leapt from the bed and threw her arms around Mrs. Veraldi, showering the startled woman with kisses and cries of "Mother! Mother! Mother!"

She dragged up a chair for Mrs. Veraldi and climbed on her lap.

"Mother," she sobbed. "It's been three years since I have seen you!"

"Pepe, how were you killed?"

Without hesitation came the reply. "We were at Gioso's Tavern—Toto, Damiano, Abele, Rosario and me. They played cards. I drank wine. After I was drunk they began to put things in the wine. Then they took me to a place near the bridge, near the Caserma di Cappussine, by the wall with the three fountains.

"Two of them, Toto and Abele, held me and shoved me through a hole in the wall. Then Rosario came through and hit me on the head. Toto struck me in the eye. Abele came up with a stone and broke my jaw. Then they took off my clothes and carried me under the bridge and Toto struck me with a piece of iron and broke my arm at the

168

wrist. They threw my clothes off the bridge and put a stone under my head so I would look crazy. But, mother, I was not so crazy that I would jump off that high bridge. I could not help myself. They were four against one and I had drunk twenty-four glasses of wine. . . . Mother, did you know that one of my killers had died in the hospital?"

Mrs. Veraldi did not know it. But subsequent investigation revealed that Abele had died in September of 1938 of a heart attack.

". . . and Toto, mother, he volunteered for service in East Africa and was badly wounded in the face. Another of the killers, Damiano, is on his way to this house right now."

Again Maria was right on all counts. Toto had left the scene of Pepe's death shortly after the funeral and had gone to East Africa (Eritrea). He never returned to Catanzaro.

Damiano had not been invited to the Talarico home but, as Maria predicted, he arrived about five minutes after she had announced his coming.

"Pepe," was ready for him. He snorted that this girl was insane, but "Pepe" began to shower him with questions about things they had done together and it was apparent that Damiano was shaken. The questions turned to the manner of Pepe's death and Damiano could only stand and shake his head. As soon as possible, he who had come only to sneer, rushed out of the house with perspiration streaming down his face. He flatly refused to be interrogated by Dr. Scambia. Damiano wanted no part of this weird and alarming turn of affairs.

During her periods of claiming to be the dead Pepe, Maria was confronted by a number of Pepe's relatives and friends to see whether she could identify them. She did so without exception, although it was certain that as Maria Talarico she had not known them and probably had never seen them.

Among them were Raffaele and Giovanni Veraldi, brothers of Pepe. She recognized both of them and called them by name as they entered the room, but refused to be friendly with Giovanni, because, she said, he did not respect their mother. A check disclosed that in the preceding week Giovanni had insulted his mother during a family argument in their home. Others whom she recognized included the owner of the Gioso Tavern, a relative of Pepe's brother-in-law, and Fabiano Luigi, a close friend of Pepe. She asked Fabiano to go to Catanzaro and get her a bologna sandwich and a bottle of brilliantine for her hair.

Fabiano was understandably surprised for he and Pepe had often gone to that same place for bologna sandwiches, and brilliantine was a favorite cosmetic that Pepe had often used.

About half an hour after Fabiano had left on this errand, Maria put down a picture she was holding and said: "Fabiano has met Biondo near the Military Hospital. They are talking about me."

When Fabiano returned, Dr. Scambia met him outside the house and questioned him about the trip. Fabiano confirmed that he had met Biondo near the hospital just as Maria had asserted, and they had talked about the peculiar activities in the Talarico house.

Maria, as Pepe, also promptly identified the picture of a dead sister of Mancuso Salvatore, a friend of Pepe. And when still another of Pepe's friends visited the Talarico home, Maria not only identified him immediately as Dell'

Apa Antonio but reminded him of the time they had worked together at the Catanzaro railroad station during the flood of 1935, a statement which Antonio told investigators was correct.

Dr. Scambia and the other medics had ample evidence that Maria Talarico had access to the memories and knowledge of the late Pepe Veraldi, while at the same time she knew nothing whatever of Maria Talarico.

Certainly one of the most puzzling aspects of the case was that involving a former Brigadier in the Italian army, Guglielmo Sita, whose testimony was set down by Dr. Scambia.

Sita, a Customs Office official at the time of the Veraldi death, had known Veraldi but did not know and had never seen Maria Talarico until he walked into her home on January 6, 1939, to test her alleged transition into Pepe Veraldi. As the Brigadier entered the house Maria said: "Let him come in. It's the Brigadier."

She then proceeded to remind him that on the night of Veraldi's death Pepe had seen him smoking his pipe in the window. This was true and Sita asked where Pepe had gone after passing Sita's house.

Maria seemed embarrassed. She got a piece of paper and passed a scribbled message to Sita. It read: "Lillina's house."

Sita knew the answer—and there it was on the slip of paper. Sita knew that Veraldi had been seeing Lillina Dellia, the pretty wife of a violently jealous neighbor of Sita. He also knew that after passing his home that fateful night, Veraldi had slipped into Lillina's, just as Maria had refused to say in the presence of others, but as she had written on the note she handed to him.

The Brigadier told Dr. Scambia that he had gone to the Talarico home a complete skeptic, but had come away badly shaken by his experience.

The bizarre case of Maria Talarico came to its end in a surprising manner. "Pepe" told Mrs. Talarico that he had a pain in his leg and must be taken at once to the bridge to get his clothes. It was explained that the clothing had been taken away by the police. Nevertheless, said "Pepe," he had to go to the bridge. After selecting four men to go with him, "Pepe" headed for the bridge with a small crowd following.

When she reached the end of the bridge, Maria never paused but began to descend the almost perpendicular bank—a dangerous feat for an experienced person and doubly dangerous for a girl who knew nothing of such feats. The four men followed her cautiously. Maria's mother, on the bridge, screamed at the men to stop her before she killed herself, but they were too preoccupied with their own risky descent to heed her cries.

Maria climbed down to the rocky river bed without difficulty. She began removing her clothing and threw the garments about her. Making her way over the stones to the exact spot where Pepe Veraldi's body had lain, she fell backward as though she had been struck with a club, her head on the same stone on which his had rested. Her right foot was bare, as his had been. She was unconscious.

The men who had followed her were understandably confused by this unexpected turn of events. They threw a coat over the girl and backed away to a respectable distance.

She lay on the cold stones for about ten minutes before she groaned and got up, evidently amazed at finding herself partially undressed in such an isolated spot with a crowd of people staring at her. Hastily putting on her garments, she was helped across the stream to an easier point of ascent and had to be assisted up the bank to the bridge level.

There, for the first time in weeks, she recognized her own mother and family. "Pepe Veraldi" was gone; she was Maria Talarico once more and as such she has remained.

When Maria learned that for more than two weeks she had been reliving the life of a man she had never known, she became ashamed and refused to leave the house. She did not recognize Dr. Scambia, who had been treating her daily during her strange experience. Later, however, she issued a statement at his request to bring an end to the gossip that still centered around her. It said:

"Of what has recently occurred, I remember nothing. You may not take my picture, for my boy friend has forbidden it. I have never even dreamed of the young fellow who was found dead under the bridge. I never talked to him or knew him. I am seventeen years old and my health has always been good. Signed, Maria Talarico, February 9, 1939."

Drs. Scambia, Fragola, Peri, Catalono and Carelli had the rare opportunity to be present at this strange case, which took place virtually at their doorsteps. Their accounts are especially reliable since many of the individuals involved were known to them as friends and as patients. A rather lengthy account is published in *La Riserca Psichica* for June, 1939, published at 6 Via Spiga, Milan, Italy.

The case of Maria Talarico demonstrates once again how little we understand of what goes on around us, within us . . . and sometimes through us.

31

The Water Witches

Finding water was a matter of life and death for so many thousands of years that the origins of water witches are lost in antiquity. Let it suffice to say that it has been believed for at least fifty centuries that, in the hands of certain persons, wands or forks from trees or bushes would react in a manner to indicate the presence of water concealed in the ground.

As man became more confident of his ability to explain everything in the light of scientific knowledge, the water witches, whom he could not explain, were dismissed as superstition and folklore, and their successes as nothing more than luck.

Water, we are told, is everywhere beneath our feet—therefore, the twisting wand which is said to point to the water is merely demonstrating the ignorance of those who use it.

That's an interesting theory and, like most theories, it has a large, economy-size hole in it. For time after time the self-styled scientific methods have been unable to locate the ubiquitous water which dowsers found with ease.

I doubt very much that General Motors Corporation

would be listed as superstitious or ignorant; yet, when they were desperate for water, they called on a dowser—after the "scientists" had failed.

In 1951, General Motors was building a huge plant at Port Elizabeth, South Africa, in semi-arid country. Big factories need dependable water supplies and this General Motors plant was no exception. (But water is everywhere underground, remember?) When it neared time for the factory to go into operation, the engineers were somewhat embarrassed. Port Elizabeth was so short of water that lawn sprinkling had been prohibited as a conservation measure. And there was no additional supply of water in sight. The only chance was a well, or wells; and dependable wells in that area are few and far between.

The corporation called in a well expert who did a lot of measuring and estimating and finally selected a site. The drillers hastily set up their gear and sent their bit in search of water. It was all very scientific and very expensive.

A middle-aged native of Port Elizabeth, C. J. Bekker, was also an employee of G. M. and he remarked to the Plant Materials Superintendent that the drillers would get nothing but a little salt water around one hundred and fifty feet—and not much of that.

When the drill tapped salt water at one hundred and fifty-five feet, Superintendent A. J. Williams recalled Bekker's remark. If Bekker knew so much about bad water— why didn't he tell them where to find good water?

Bekker did not resort to the old willow wand as most dowsers do. Instead, he simply folded his arms akimbo tightly across his chest and began walking slowly back and forth across the sprawling G. M. property. After half an hour, he came to a halt and motioned the officials to mark the spot where he stood, vibrating rather violently. "Here," said Bekker through chattering teeth, "I am standing over a large stream of fresh water—good water that we can use." After the spot was properly marked, Bekker continued his slow pacing until he again began to shiver and shake at another spot about eighteen hundred feet from the first, and again the place was marked.

The G. M. plant officials were in a quandry. They had invited the man to conduct the experiment; but, as they all knew, it was nothing more than superstition. Should they spend Company funds on such nonsense?

Someone suggested that they cross-check by blindfolding Bekker and having him conduct the same tests again. He was quite willing and permitted them to cover his eyes tightly. Then two of the officials led him back and forth across the property again—and again Bekker got the same reaction at the same spots, almost in the same footprints he had made before. Certainly he didn't need to see in order to get the reaction, whatever it was.

General Motors funds went into the drilling of a well at a spot indicated by a dowser. The money was well spent; for there was plenty of fresh water there; enough for the factory and enough for keeping the lawns and flowers fresh and green. There was, in fact, such an ample supply in that first well that there was no need to drill the second.

For C. J. Bekker it was an old story. He had been born in the arid Jansenville district about a hundred miles from Port Elizabeth and the farmers there had to find water or go broke. Bekker's grandfather was in demand as a dowser and it was he who taught his grandson his method, of folding his arms across his chest and walking slowly back and forth until the shivering starts.

General Motors was so happy with its unusual method of finding the well at Port Elizabeth that it wrote up the full story of the incident in its Company magazine *General Motors Folks* for October, 1951.

In describing his methods, Bekker says:

"I find that I can distinguish between fresh and salt water by holding a silver coin in one hand and a copper coin in the other. Fresh water underground causes the hand containing the silver coin to vibrate rather violently, but if the copper coin vibrates I know the water is salt. It always works for me although I don't know why."

Bekker told the G. M. officials that he had noticed several interesting peculiarities about his technique.

"For one thing," he said, "if I am standing over a subterranean stream, vibrating as I do, and unlock my hands, the vibration stops instantly. Also, if I face in the direction of the underground flow, the vibration will stop; but if I face upstream the effect on me is instantaneous and violent, and seems to be governed to a large extent by the strength of the flow.

"I have found, I believe, that there are three distinct currents or whatever they can be called, that come from the underground water. One comes straight up and the others go off at angles of forty-five degrees. When I am getting the most severe vibration, I know that I am directly above the center of the stream. I then walk back and forth until I can feel the furthest reaction point on each side. By simply counting my paces I can tell the depth of the stream, just as I did at General Motors."

On one parched farm near Port Elizabeth, where twelve drill holes had found nothing, Bekker brought in a heavy flow of sweet water at the first try. On the farm of a

Mr. Carelse, Bekker located a fast-flowing stream about four hundred feet down. The fourteen-foot strip in the center of the stream had such a powerful reaction on him that Bekker was frequently flung to the ground as he tried to cross that portion. Drilling confirmed his findings, as it has ninety-eight per cent of the time.

The dowsing, you see, is just superstition, but the water is very real indeed and Bekker is in demand for the simple reason that he gets results.

Results were much in demand in Kennewick, Washington, in 1956 when the authorities set out to find some lost underground utility pipes. All the maps were either missing or misleading and digging for the pipes was not only prohibitive but required time which was not available.

City Engineer Marston B. Winegar solved the problem through his ability as a dowser. Some time before, Superintendent Harry Ray had heard about a dowsing device made of two one-quarter-inch welding rods, fitted loosely into a couple of sleeves made of copper tubing. Mr. Ray had first heard of the rods being used in Eugene, Oregon, and he had a set made for himself, to be used in laying mains for the Cascade Natural Gas Company.

Trouble was, they would not work for Mr. Ray, so Mr. Winegar decided to try them. He discovered that for him they showed surprising activity.

He holds a rod in each hand parallel to the ground and pointing straight ahead. As he walks across a buried pipeline, the rods twist around to parallel the direction of the pipe. He says: "There is no particular sensation involved, other than surprise, but it works."

He first began using the rods in the winter of 1955 and, since that time, many other persons have tried them.

About half of those who tried found that they got results—the others found them unresponsive.

The American Water Works Association has published literature on how to use welding rods for this purpose. It is interesting to note that the rods will not work on concrete or wooden pipes, although many have tried them. Why don't they work under those conditions? Or better still, why *do* they work on metal pipes?

In the U. S. Department of Agriculture Yearbook devoted to water, the U. S. Geological Survey says:

"It is doubtful whether so much investigation and discussion have been bestowed on any other subject with such absolute lack of positive results."

That statement was written by Arthur Sowder.

Arthur Sowder is a dowser.

While the dowsers find fresh water, their detractors find fresh alibis.

The members of a rural School Board near Bloomington, Illinois, found their institution short of water in the spring of 1956 so they had the conventional geological studies made, hired some expert well drillers and waited for results. They got some excellent dry holes for their money.

Across the road from the school lived Mrs. J. M. Curry. Would she permit them to drill for water on her property? Her answer was polite, but firm and negative. But Mrs. Curry made them an interesting counteroffer: She would "witch" them some water on *their* property if they liked. What could they lose?

Mrs. Curry went into her orchard and cut a fork from a peach tree. With this she strolled back and forth across the school property until she finally selected a spot where she told them they would find water, not much deeper than seventy feet. The Board members thanked her but they did not drill.

Instead, one of the Board members got in touch with a friend of his who was reputedly able to find water by witching. Oddly, this friend selected a spot which was only a foot from that which Mrs. Curry had chosen, although the friend had known nothing of her efforts. A third dowser was called in, and when his willow wand indicated water right where the others had made their marks, the School Board began to wonder if they were overlooking something. Mrs. Curry had told them there was water "not much deeper than seventy feet." The second dowser had estimated it at eighty feet. The third dowser selected the same spot as his predecessors and predicted water at "about seventy-five feet." So the School Board pondered and procrastinated for a few days before they went out and secured the services of a *fourth* dowser!

That did it.

Dowser number four located a spot less than three feet from the other three. The befuddled School Board put the drillers back to work and the well came in at eighty-six feet. It is a dependable well, in gravel, located right where all four "water-witchers" had marked their spots—a well located by the "folklore, ignorance and superstition" of dowsing.

In spite of their frequent successes, it must be kept in mind that dowsers are not infallible. For instance, there is a chap named Carl Windrum, proprietor of a hardware store in Dawson, Nebraska, who regards his dowsing as a sort of hobby. In a ten-year period, 1950-1960, he dowsed forty wells and only thirty-nine of them produced adequate

180

amounts of water. Mr. Windrum, let it be noted, does not use the conventional peach forks or willow wands. He prefers a forked elm stick and, when he crosses a subterranean water vein, the elm fork, he says, turns upside down. How deep is the vein? Mr. Windrum says he has only to hold the same stick upright and it bobs slowly up and down. Each "bob" is counted as approximately one foot, the total indicating the depth of the well. Students of such things will recall that this is substantially the method used by Henry Gross, probably the best known of all the dowsers, thanks to the book *Henry Gross and his Dowsing Rod.*

Some dowsers appear to be able to use their much-maligned techniques to detect substances other than water. Among the best documented instances of such uses is that which was widely reported by the Canadian Press in July of 1956.

For two years the engineers had been baffled by a subterranean oil leak that was playing havoc with the homes of Owen Niblett and Lyle Watson in Toronto. Little by little the stench in the homes worsened until both houses smelled like oil refineries. The gaseous aroma was so strong that they were advised not to light any fires.

Finally, after the frustrated and embarrassed engineers admitted they could not explain the phenomenon, and after Niblett's house began to sink on one side, the engineers called in a local dowser, Mrs. Beatrice Sprowl. Did she think she could locate the presence and path of underground oil as she claimed to be able to do with water?

Mrs. Sprowl admittedly did not know—but she was willing to try. Even if she failed it would not make matters worse.

Taking her freshly-cut forked switch in her hands, Mrs. Sprowl began to circle the houses. Presently she found a spot where the wand seemed to be unusually active and from there she began branching out until she seemed to find a pattern that led her across a nearby highway. Zigzagging developed a path that took her on across two township roads, over a railway track and through a broad hayfield. In her hands the contortions of the forked switch varied as she crossed and recrossed the apparent line of oil seepage. Suddenly she stopped, circled the spot and marked it for the engineers. They dug where she had indicated and found two high-pressure oil transmission lines, leaking merrily into the spongy sub-strata, which had finally carried the unprocessed crude beneath the homes of the long-suffering Nibletts and Watsons.

Mrs. Sprowl, using only the ridiculous and impossible techniques of the dowsers, had found the source of the trouble which the engineers had been unable to locate after two years of scientific searching. She found it in two hours and twenty minutes.

32

The Remarkable Rainmakers

Man's efforts to control the weather have embraced a wide variety of methods. In the early days of the human race and in some outposts to the present day, the witch doctors peer into a puddle of chicken entrails and mutter magic words to coax the clouds to disgorge. If it rains, they take credit. If it doesn't rain, they blame it on what the broadcasting industry refers to as "circumstances beyond our control."

Some shaman, sharper than his contemporaries, probably noticed that great rains followed great forest fires. But starting forest fires was restricted to certain areas and was just as likely to roast the medicine man as to cover him with rain and glory. Yet there *did* seem to be a relationship between smoke and rain.

It got some attention from the great scholars when men began settling their international disputes with gunpowder, and especially with cannon. It seemed that each great battle was followed by a gully-washer rain. Soldiers of the line, short on education but long on practicality, noticed that the clouds of white cannon smoke which soared heavenward were soon joined by great rolling thunderheads, and where there had been blue sky at the beginning of the battle there was later lightning and wind and rain. Was there a relationship?

During our own Civil War rains followed the use of massed artillery with such frequency that the soldiers accepted the rain as a natural concomitant of battle and in their letters referred to them as "battle storms." And, if the battle was held on a day when there was little or no wind, it seemed to the soldiers that the ensuing storms were especially violent. Perhaps it was just coincidence that the rain followed the battles. Perhaps it was because battles were fought on fair days and fair days are followed by rains, battle or no. Perhaps.

In the decade preceding the advent of the Twentieth Century, an Australian named Frank Melbourne came to this country and advertised himself as a professional rainmaker. His formula was secret, of course. When Frank was on the job he set up a high canvas wall around an area about thirty feet square and permitted no one inside the secret zone but himself. Into huge iron vats he poured his chemicals and presently the fumes would begin to roll heavenward, directed for the first thirty feet by a metal smokestack.

Goodland, Kansas, was gasping for water in 1891. The farmers scraped together and hired Frank Melbourne to break the drought. He set up his gear in a shallow depression that had once been a pond and sent his secret fog into the blue. When he started there wasn't a cloud in the sky and there had been none for days—but by midafternoon the clouds were thick and dark and by nightfall the jubilant farmers were standing out in the deluge, getting soaked with the best news they had had in weeks. Some bankers formed a little company and induced Melbourne to sell them his formula, for part of the profits. The company entered into scores of agreements to make rain; no rain, no pay. Then came a wet year and Melbourne was last heard of in Africa where, someone had told him, a rainmaker could still make a fortune.

Melbourne may have left a bit too soon, for the perusal of Kansas papers shows that he was succeeded in 1893 by an enterprising train dispatcher named C. B. Jewell, whose technique was not only equal to Melbourne's in effectiveness but was immeasurably more spectacular. Mr. Jewell would tie a bundle of dynamite to the underside of a small captive balloon, run it up about five hundred to a thousand feet and detonate the explosive by a telegraph wire.

He explained that by transferring the blast directly to the heavens he got the same results with less explosives. Battles jarred the heavens with concussion waves reflected from the earth, he said, while he jarred the heavens by direct contact.

Mr. Jewell pleased the public with his midday fireworks and he pleased the farmers with the floods that gushed from the skies to replenish their ponds and cisterns. He later added still another bit of business to his rainmaking procedure—that of generating gas in huge stone jars, tickling it with some electricity until it sizzled and then sending the fumes aloft to "disrupt the equilibrium of the skies," as he described it.

The Rock Island Railroad was suffering along with the farmers; for, when the farmers had nothing to ship, the railroad had nothing to haul. If this fellow Jewell really could make it rain, he was a godsend to the railroad, too, and they cautiously offered him free transportation to help him conduct his work—along their railroad, of course.

With free rail transportation and three big flatcars to hold his gear, C. B. Jewell proceeded in style from one parched community along the Rock Island to the next. Gradually, rain followed his dabbling with the nauseous vapors. Trouble was, sometimes there was too much rain and in that case Jewell admitted he was helpless. "I can turn it on," he told a committee of irate farmers whose crops were sliding down the creeks, "but no man alive can turn off a rainstorm!"

Perhaps his most spectacular demonstration was the one he gave near Wichita. For weeks the dust devils had been chasing each other through the nearly bald wheat fields. The beleaguered farmers, faced with bankruptcy or worse, sent for Jewell. When he arrived on his three flatcars, the editors of the Wichita papers greeted him with hoots of derision. They cited one eminent scientist after another to support their contention that rainmakers were frauds and those who hired them were something less than intelligent.

The former train-dispatcher-turned-rainmaker bore the rude greeting with his customary calm, for he had had plenty of experience with such matters in the past. After he got his gear set up in a farm a few miles from Wichita, he sent word to one of the most vociferous of the journalists that he was going to turn Wichita's main street into a river.

Twenty-four hours later rivers and creeks were out of their banks and the rain was falling in torrents. Jewell didn't quite get the river up to the main street but it did get high enough for public opinion to swing to his side. The nasty editorials vanished from the presses.

Probably the best known, best loved and best remembered of the native rainmakers was Charles Mallory Hatfield. As a boy on his father's farm near San Diego, he knew of the legendary exploits of "Prophet" Potts, who billed himself as a precipitator and who operated in southern California shortly before the turn of the century. Hatfield said that Potts stimulated his boyish interest and it remained only for seed to be scattered on such fertile soil. That happened the day that Hatfield came upon a copy of a book by Edward Powers, written in 1871, and dealing with the "science of pluviculture." Powers contended that rain could be coaxed from the skies by scientific methods. His volume attracted so much attention that Congress appropriated money in 1891 to conduct an official investigation and numerous tests of Powers' theory.

Charles Mallory Hatfield had anticipated them there— he was already conducting his own experiments and was doing it with the fervor of a dedicated man, which indeed he was.

By 1902 he was so far along with his experiments that he gave up his job as a sewing machine salesman and plunged full-time into the career of rainmaking. His procedure, like that of Melbourne and Jewell before him, consisted of getting fumes into the atmosphere. Hatfield built a large wooden tank that stood on stout wooden legs which held the tanks about twelve feet above the ground. He dumped his chemicals into the tanks, stirred them until well mixed, poured in some water and a few gallons of acid, clapped a wooden lid on the tank and scrambled down. After a wait of about twenty minutes, Hatfield would lift the lid from the tank with a long pole and watch the clouds of evil-smelling vapor spiral toward the sky.

Hatfield was a quiet and extremely modest man. He never claimed that he could make rain; he merely contended that he assisted nature. How? By overturning the balance of the atmosphere so that the moisture was focused instead of being dispersed, he would reply.

His first commercial contract was a fifty-dollar agreement to "precipitate moisture" for a farmer near Los Angeles in 1903. Much to the astonishment of all who watched him set up his tanks, the vapors were followed by an inch of rain and the overjoyed farmer gave Hatfield an extra fifty dollars to show his appreciation.

Altogether, he discharged more than five hundred rainmaking contracts in and around Los Angeles in a period of twenty-five years, the fees ranging from fifty to ten thousand dollars. For four thousand dollars he agreed to fill the Lake Hemet reservoir. His experiments were promptly followed by eleven inches of rain, which raised the water level in the reservoir by twenty-two feet and gave the operators of it the biggest bargain they ever had, according to their own testimony.

Hatfield roamed far and wide with his chemicals and his evaporation tanks. In 1906, when the Klondike streams were so dry the miners could not work their sluice boxes, they sent for Hatfield. The miners at Dawson City gave him ten thousand dollars in gold to come to their rescue. They got what they ordered, for thirty-six hours after Hatfield went into action, the storm clouds were rolling and the four inches of rain he brought were more than enough.

In 1922 a terrible drought brought distress and ruin to southern Italy. The Government sought aid from Hatfield and he went immediately. To fail would have spelled ruin —but Hatfield did not fail. In the wake of his efforts, torrential rains filled every reservoir and brought new life to the parched fields. He was a national hero whose picture was on the front page of every Italian paper.

From Italy to Alaska and from Canada to Argentina, Hatfield and his evaporators went about upsetting the balance of nature with the mystic vapors. At Randsburg, in the desolate Mohave Desert, Hatfield's vapors were followed by an incredible *forty inches of rain* in three hours, a spectacle never before duplicated there and never equalled since. It was his smashing reply to an attack by the noted educator, David Starr Jordan, who claimed that Hatfield always waited until the drought was nearly over before he went to work. Hatfield took the newsmen into the Mohave Desert, where the drought was never over, and delivered a deluge to which Dr. Jordan had no reply.

Death came to the old rainmaker on January 22, 1958, at the age of eighty-two, at his home in Pearblossom, California. He had lived to see this nation spend millions of dollars in rainmaking experiments, some of which seemed to duplicate his own techniques. In 1951, Dr. Irving Langmuir concluded a long series of such experiments for the Navy and said to newsmen: "I can send up silver iodide fumes in New Mexico and make it rain all the way to Michigan!"

When Michigan resort owners recalled the unseasonal

rains that had crippled business that year, they raised such a rumpus that the Navy denied everything and Dr. Langmuir suddenly became mute on the subject. Verily, the way of the rainmaker is hard.

By the time of Hatfield's death in 1958, rainmaking had become a respectable field of scientific endeavor. By sending aloft minute particles of silver iodide or other chemicals, the scientists discovered that they could induce the formation of tiny droplets, focusing the moisture that is in the air and upsetting the balance of nature, as Hatfield had called it.

Charles Mallory Hatfield, the rainmaker who never claimed to be one, had lived long enough to see his explanations vindicated and his techniques used as the basis of a new science, now called weather control. He never got any credit, of course, and he never expected any.

Hatfield was always willing to settle for a good cloudburst.

33

Chorus For Catastrophe

A strange incident involving a dream began one evening in the spring of 1912, when the minister of the Rosedale Methodist Church in Winnipeg, Canada, sat down for a little nap before the services. He could not have slept more than twenty minutes but, during that time, the Reverend Charles Morgan dreamed the same thing repeatedly. Against a great sound of rushing waters and a tumult of excited voices, he heard the words of an old song that he had not heard in many years.

It was such a strange and disturbing experience that he could not dismiss it from his mind. At the conclusion of the regular services that evening he told the congregation of his unusual dream and asked them to sing with him the old hymn which he had heard during the dream, a song which says, "Hear, Father, while we pray to Thee for those in peril on the sea."

The headlines in the newspapers the next morning only deepened the mystery for, at the same moment that the Reverend Morgan was having that strange dream in Winnipeg, one of the great ocean tragedies of all times was occurring in the icy waters of the North Atlantic—the sinking of the Titanic.

34

The Prime
Minister's Dream

Through the magic of dreams, the individual seems to be able to annihilate distance and to disregard time. This is not true of everyone, of course, but it is true of many favored individuals—and some are not always aware of their gift.

Dreams often lead to some surprising results—to events which coincide with the dream sequences so closely that the dream itself seems to have been a preview.

One morning in 1812 the Prime Minister of England, Spencer Perceval, told his family of a disturbing dream he had had the night before. In this dream, he said, he had been walking through the lobby of the House of Commons when he suddenly was confronted by a crazed individual brandishing a pistol. The man was wearing a dark green coat with shiny brass buttons. Without warning, the intruder pointed the pistol at the Prime Minister and fired. Then everything had gone black, which Perceval decided must have indicated that he had been killed.

Surpassingly strange was the experience of a wealthy gentleman, John Williams, who had the same dream Spencer Perceval had, but he had it seven days before Perceval's dream.

On May 3, 1812, Williams was living on his estate in

Redruth, Cornwall. He had little interest in politics but that night he dreamed that he was standing in the cloakroom of the House of Commons when a small man in a dark green coat whipped out a pistol and shot another man in the breast. The victim slumped to the floor and quickly died. Upon inquiry, Williams was told that the slain man was Prime Minister Spencer Perceval.

Williams woke up and told his wife of the nightmare. He went back to sleep and dreamed the same thing over again. Again he awakened and shortly before morning he dropped off to sleep, only to experience the same dream for the third time.

It disturbed him to such an extent that he discussed it with friends. Should he go to London and warn the Prime Minister? Should he try to send him a letter and tell him of the alarming dream? When his friends laughed at him for being so disturbed about a dream, Williams gave up the idea.

Williams had his series of dreams during the night of May 3-4. Perceval had the same dream on the night of May 10-11. When the Prime Minister related his dream to his family that morning, they pleaded with him not to attend that day's session. But he felt that his presence was necessary and that he was not justified in remaining home by anything so insubstantial as a disturbing dream.

As Prime Minister Perceval walked through the lobby of the House of Commons on the morning of May 11, 1812, a bushy haired man whom he had never seen before stepped from behind a pillar and shot him to death.

The killer was a madman who fancied he had a grievance against the government. He was wearing a dark green coat with shiny brass buttons.

35

Strange Dreams
That Came True

Rudyard Kipling delighted in recounting to friends a peculiar little dream that he had—and for which he could find no explanation.

He dreamed that he was dressed in formal attire and that he was attending some function in a vast hall which had rough stone slabs for flooring. He was being jostled around by a throng of men, who were also formally dressed. He was aware that a ceremony was in progress but he could not see what was going on because of a fat man's stomach which blocked his view. At the close of the ceremony the crowd began moving toward the front of the hall. Just then a man stepped out of the throng and grasped Kipling by the arm and said: "I want a word with you."

It was about six weeks later when Kipling was attending an official gathering that he realized that the scene was exactly like the ceremony in his dream. There were the throng of men in formal dress, the rough stone slab floor and a fat man's stomach was obstructing his view as its owner stood on a stairway slightly above Kipling.

As he was wondering how far the coincidence would go,

the ceremony ended and everyone began to move forward. Just then a total stranger stepped out of the crowd and grasped his sleeve. Kipling turned and the man said, "May I have a word with you?"

The stranger's mission was inconsequential but the incident was of eerie interest to Kipling because it happened exactly as he had seen it in his dream.

In October of 1918, Robert Beresford was a four-year-old youngster in Buckinghamshire, England. World War I was grinding to its finale, but that was of little interest to four-year-old boys.

On the afternoon of October 11, while Bobbie was taking his customary nap, he began muttering in his sleep. It was something the child had never done before and his father, Jamie, bent down to listen. He heard Bobbie saying, again and again, "Oh, poor Mrs. Timms! Poor Mrs. Timms! Won't someone please tell her?"

Neither of Bobbie's parents knew anyone named Timms and they couldn't imagine what he was talking about, nor why he should bemoan the plight of someone he did not know. The parents called the family doctor who was passing by, and he too was baffled by what he heard. The doctor asked Bobbie why Mrs. Timms should be told—what was the message?

For a couple of minutes there was silence, broken only by the child's labored breathing; then he muttered:

"It's about Edwin! He's dead . . . dead in the mud! Oh, poor Mrs. Timms!"

When four-year-old Bobbie awakened, he seemed quite normal and did not recall any dream at all.

And what of poor Mrs. Timms?

The doctor's wife finally recalled that a lady by that

name lived in a village about twenty miles distant and, upon investigation, they learned that she did have a son named Edwin, who was then with the British forces in France.

Three days after the little boy's dream, Mrs. Timms received notice that her son had been killed in battle . . . and his death had occurred the day before Bobbie Beresford had muttered that Edwin was dead.

Somehow, in his sleep, the child had been talking about two people he had never heard of, and their relationship to an event that transpired two hundred miles away.

James Watt is best remembered as the inventor of the first practical steam engine, a machine which helped revolutionize the civilized world. But Mr. Watt also made another contribution, less dramatic than the steam engine but equally lasting, and he attributed it to a dream.

In his day, the making of lead shot for shotguns was an involved and costly process. Lead was rolled into sheets and the sheets were chopped into bits, or the lead was drawn into wire which was then cut into short segments. In either case its performance was unpredictable and its price was prohibitive.

That's how it was when Mr. Watt began having the same dream, night after night, for a week. According to his own account of the experience, he seemed to be walking along in a heavy rainstorm, but instead of rain he was being showered with tiny leaden pellets that rolled about his feet. Was it significant? Did this mean that molten lead falling through the air would harden into tiny spherical pellets?

Watt got permission to make an experiment in the

tower of a church which had a water-filled moat at its base. He melted a few pounds of lead and tossed it out of the belfry. When he recovered it from the water in the moat, he found to his delight that it had indeed hardened into tiny globules. From that day to this, all lead shot has been made by the process which was discovered by James Watt, thanks to his remarkable dreams.

At the disaster of Dunkirk in 1940, one of the missing men was Corporal Teddy Watson, whose mother, Mrs. Helen Watson, lived at Ellerbuck, England. It was a virtual certainty that her son was dead; but, if he was, the military had no record of his burial, since many of the records had been lost in that evacuation from Dunkirk.

In 1956, realizing that she probably would not live much longer, Mrs. Watson repeatedly wished that she could find her son's grave. As if in answer to her longing, she had a vivid dream in which she entered a military cemetery with hundreds of white crosses. She walked along slowly until she came to a cross near the corner of the cemetery. There her son appeared, smiled, and vanished.

Mrs. Watson had seen a landmark by which she felt that she could identify the cemetery. She went to Dunkirk and quickly located the spot, just as she had seen it in her dream. When she came to the cross beside which her son seemed to have appeared, she pointed it out to the officer who had accompanied her and he made a note of the location.

When she got back to England, there was a message waiting for her. The grave she had pointed out had been opened. The rosary, the monogrammed cigarette holder and the picture in the locket were those of her son.

36

The Boy Who Returned From The Grave

Max Hoffman was a five-year-old in 1865 when he came down with cholera. The family doctor came out to the farm near a small Wisconsin town and, after examining the child, gave the parents no hope for his recovery.

The illness had raged only three days when little Max died and was buried in the village cemetery.

The next night the child's mother had a terrifying nightmare. She dreamed that Max had turned over in his coffin and seemed to be struggling to escape. She saw his hands clasped under his right cheek. The mother woke up screaming. She implored her husband to dig up the child's coffin—but he refused. Mr. Hoffman felt that her dream was the result of the emotional strain they had undergone and that digging up the body would only renew the agony.

But the next night it happened again and this time the frantic mother would not be ignored. Hoffman sent one of the eldest children to bring a neighbor and a lantern, since his own lantern was broken.

Shortly after one o'clock in the morning, the men began

the task of exhuming the child's coffin. They worked by the light of a lantern that swayed from the limb of a nearby tree. When they finally got the box out on the sod and pried off the lid, they found that Max's body was twisted to the right, just as his mother had dreamed, and under his right cheek his hands had made indentations.

There was no sign of life in the little fellow but Mr. Hoffman took the body in his arms and rode horseback to the home of the doctor. With considerable misgiving, the physician went to work trying to revive the child he had pronounced dead two days before. After more than an hour of work they were rewarded by the flicker of an eyelid. Brandy was administered, heated salt bags were placed under the child's arms. Little by little, hour after hour, signs of improvement could be noted.

Within a week Max Hoffman had fully recovered from his fantastic experience. He lived well into his eighties at Clinton, Iowa, and among his most prized possessions were the little metal handles off the coffin from which he was rescued by his mother's dream.

37

A Prehistoric Dream

Henry Field, was a close personal friend of Joseph Mandemant. Both men were eminent figures in the field of anthropology. Both men knew how frustrating their searches could be, and how easily they might overlook the find of the century by failing to look in precisely the right place. Mandemant, says Field, had the priceless knack of being able to put his subconscious to work for him, sometimes with incredible results.

One night, during the course of a particularly vivid dream, Mandemant found himself looking into the entrance of a cavern which he instantly recognized as the Bedeilhac cave in France. It was night in his dream and he could make out clearly the group of Magdalenian hunters squatting around their campfire a short distance inside the mouth of the cave. Among other things, Mandemant noticed drawings of hunting scenes on the roof of the cavern, dimly lighted by the flickering campfire.

Sitting apart from the others in the cave were a young couple, clad in skins like the others. Mandemant guessed that they were lovers. The male rose and led the girl into a short, dark cleft which led into a side room and to a ledge. Although their rendezvous was almost totally dark, Mandemant could hear their whispers and could dimly see the boy stroking the long shiny hair of his companion. Suddenly there was a terrible grinding roar as the stony roof of the cave tore asunder and came crashing down, sealing off that portion in which the young couple had concealed themselves.

Mandemant was so impressed by the dream that he wrote it down in detail and placed the description in a bank vault. Then he proceeded to the cave at Bedeilhac. It looked just as it had in his dream, except that the right wall of the first great "room" appeared to be solid limestone. The noted French scientist admittedly felt that he was on a wild goose chase, for there was no sign of the cleft which had enabled the young couple in his dream to enter the side cavern. Mandemant rapped on the wall with a mallet . . . and the sound that came back was encouragingly hollow.

Workmen were hired and put to the task of breaking a hole through the great stone slab, a task that took several days. At last they got through. There was the cleft, just as the scientist had described it from his dream. He squeezed through the passageway into the next cavern. There was the ledge on which he had dreamed of seeing the Stone Age lovers—but the ledge was empty.

Examination of the outer cavern showed that the rock fall which had shattered his dream (and the lovers' tryst) had consisted of a great sheet of stone from the roof of the outer cave—the slab his workmen had to break their way through, leaving a crevice between the slab and the wall of the outer room through which the young couple could have escaped.

Mandemant was disappointed at finding the cavern empty where his dream had led him to believe he might find human remains of great antiquity. Yet the dream had shown him the existence and location of an unsuspected passageway and a side cavern with the ledge. Then he remembered the hunting scenes on the roof of still another cavern room. Were they really there?

Retracing the steps of his dreams, Mandemant led his crew to the long, low-roofed cave room where he had seen the drawings. There, deep inside the cave, were the drawings he had described, crude hunting scenes smoked and etched by the skin-clad dawn men whom he had seen in his dream that spanned thousands of years of time.

PART
THREE

38

The Remarkable Edgar Cayce

Readers of *The New York Times* must have been surprised to find in their Sunday Magazine the headline "Illiterate Man Becomes Doctor When Hypnotized —Strange Power Shown by Edgar Cayce Puzzles Physicians." The article continued: "The medical fraternity of the county is taking a lively interest in the strange power said to be possessed by Edgar Cayce of Hopkinsville, Ky., to diagnose difficult diseases while in a semi-conscious state, though he has not the slightest knowledge of medicine when not in this condition."

The article, complete with pictures of Cayce, his father and of Dr. Wesley Ketchum, who assisted in the unusual demonstrations, ran in the *Times* on October 9, 1910, and was evidently based, with slight misconceptions, on a report which Dr. Ketchum had sent to the American Society of Clinical Research in Boston.

In its essentials, the article carried in the *Times* was quite correct and altogether astounding.

Mr. Cayce was by no means illiterate; he had finished

nine grades of schooling at a country school near Hopkinsville. He was in his school days, as in the balance of
his life, a quiet, unassuming, patient and congenial fellow.

The first indication that Edgar might be somewhat out
of the ordinary came when he was about nine years old.
He had found himself unable to spell "cabin"— a predicament which brought giggles from his classmates and a
sharp reprimand from his uncle Lucian, the teacher. When
Edgar reached home after school he found that Uncle
Lucian had preceded him; his father, Squire Cayce, was
both humiliated and angry.

There followed, that evening in the Cayce parlor, a
distressing scene during which the father tried to instill in
his son some understanding of the rudiments of spelling
and the boy seemed unable, or unwilling, to learn. By ten
o'clock the paternal patience was exhausted. The Squire
boxed Edgar so hard the boy fell off his chair. As he lay
on the floor, Edgar said later, he heard a voice that said:
"If you can sleep a little, we can help you." Who it was
or where it came from he did not know, but he says he
heard it clearly.

Edgar asked his father for a respite and the parent
replied the he was going into the kitchen for a few
minutes (probably to regain his composure) and that when
he returned they were going to resume their study—and
Edgar had better show some signs of intelligence.

When the father returned, he found Edgar sound asleep
with his spelling book tucked under his head. Mr. Cayce
later estimated that he had been out of the room not more
than fifteen minutes. Angry at this turn of events, he jerked
the book from under the boy's head and shook him awake.

Edgar told his father that he knew the lesson now—and

much to the parent's surprise—Edgar *did* know it. Not only that lesson but every lesson in the book!

At first Squire Cayce was angry, for he suspected that his son had known the lessons all the time and had been pretending that he didn't. The father bowled the boy over again with a resounding wallop and ordered him to bed. Edgar went willingly, of course, and jubilantly, for he had discovered an unsuspected trait that never deserted him. He had only to sleep on a book and he could thereafter quote it verbatim.

Much to Uncle Lucian's surprise, Edgar became a top student, literally overnight. He seemed to know everything in the books. His puzzled father inquired about this sudden burst of brilliance and Edgar told him about the "voice"—and the acquisition of learning while he slept.

Squire Casey was puzzled; and, as the years went by, he found himself in distinguished company. For scores of learned men came and saw and listened, and they too were puzzled.

According to the family, Edgar first evidenced the trait that was to make him famous when he was sixteen, his last year in school. During a game on the schoolhouse lawn, Edgar was struck on the spine by a hard baseball and went home dazed and irrational. His parents put him to bed, where he suddenly became serious and authoritative, ordering his mother to prepare a poultice to be applied to the spot where the ball had struck him. It was done, and next morning he was quite normal and remembered nothing of the events that had transpired from the moment he had been struck.

So many peculiar things centered about the boy that by this time Edgar Cayce was regarded by the community as something af an odd ball. He was well liked, all right, but he was also shunned as a sort of freak.

It should be understood that Squire Cayce was largely responsible for this state of affairs; for he lost few opportunities to spread the word of Edgar's wild talents. The Squire was no windbag and he had no need to exaggerate; the facts were sufficiently incredible. Edgar provided the clincher for his proud father's stories when he repeated verbatim a speech written by a local politician, a speech that lasted an hour and a half. He had merely slept with it under his head the night before.

As a young man in Hopkinsville, Cayce clerked in a dry goods store, moved on to a similar job in a Louisville book store and in early 1900 went out as a salesman for an insurance company. He contracted a throat ailment which refused to respond to treatment and came home disheartened and crushed. The doctors had told him he would never again speak above a whisper.

Edgar attended a stage show at which a professional hypnotist played to packed houses with his routine of mystifying and laugh-getting stunts. After the performance the hypnotist, who had heard of Edgar's plight, tried to relieve it through post-hypnotic suggestion, only to find himself baffled when Cayce refused to go into the deep sleep which must precede the suggestion. The hypnotist enlisted the interest of a celebrated New York medical practitioner who dabbled in hypnotism, but the medic's visit to Hopkinsville was also a failure as far as Cayce's hoarseness was concerned. The doctor went away, defeated.

Desperate, Edgar Cayce turned to a local amateur hypnotist, Al Layne, for advice. On a Sunday afternoon in March of 1901, in the parlor of Squire Cayce's home, they conducted the experiment that was to direct Edgar Cayce into his life work.

Actually it was Edgar who put himself to sleep, with Layne and his own parents standing by to do what they could. Edgar closed his eyes. His breathing deepened. When Layne was certain that Cayce was in a trance-like condition he began to describe the ailment that had bothered the patient so long. He and Edgar had agreed that, since Edgar could not, or would not, accept post-hypnotic suggestions from others, he might possibly originate such suggestions for himself while under hypnosis.

Suddenly the sick man spoke in a voice as clear and unaffected as it had ever been.

He said: "Yes. We can see the body."

Slowly and coherently he described the conditions which had caused a partial paralysis of the vocal cords. This, he said, could be cured by restoring increased circulation to the inoperative muscles and nerves.

During the next twenty minutes his upper chest and throat turned a fiery red. At Edgar's instructions, Layne ordered the circulation to return to normal. When he awakened Cayce a few moments later, they found his voice fully restored.

It was the beginning of a strange career that lasted forty-five years.

When word of this latest Cayce "miracle" spread, he found himself deluged with requests for helping others as he had helped himself. Edgar, being the obliging fellow that he was, was willing to try but also reluctant, lest he only make matters worse. After all he was dealing in human lives; he, who had no medical training whatever was presuming to tell the professional medics what to do. And predicating all of it on nothing more substantial than the ability to put himself to sleep and to have his words recorded while he was in that condition.

At first with Layne standing by—and later with medical doctors participating—Cayce began his strange career. Always, while he was in a self-induced trance, and after the patient's condition had been described to him—would come the words: "Yes. We have the body here." Then the diagnosis, couched in medical terminology indicative of extensive training and experience, and that would be followed by a prescription for treatment.

From the outset, Cayce and his fellow workers insisted that the treatments be administered by local doctors who had access to the patients. This was not always done, sometimes because the doctors refused to be associated with such a bizarre program and sometimes because the patients were so disgusted with their local medics that they simply ignored them. Then, again, many of the prescriptions that emanated from Cayce's trances were simplicity itself: gargles, poultices, exercises, plasters and home-made teas and tonics. There was frequent recourse to osteopathy and especially to that phase of it which is best known today as chiropractic manipulation—the manipulation of the spine to restore free flow of nerve energy throughout the body.

As the word of what Cayce was doing spread, first through an article in the Bowling Green, Kentucky, paper in 1903 and later through Louisville and Nashville papers, the incoming mail, telegrams and long-distance telephone calls became a seven-day-a-week torrent.

Because he took no fees for his services, Edgar Cayce was hard put to make a living. Now married and working as a photographer's assistant, he was unable to make ends meet. On January 1, 1906, Edgar spent the day in an unheated furniture factory taking pictures and that evening he collapsed in his studio. A doctor was called, and another and another until the studio contained half a dozen of them. Unable to detect a pulse, they broke out some of his teeth trying to force brandy down his throat. One medic gave Cayce an injection of morphine, another then adminstered strychnine and still another gave him another injection of morphine!

If he was not dead when they first went to work on him he should certainly have been dead by the time they finished their ministrations.

An hour after the doctors had gone, convinced that he was dead, Cayce regained consciousness and demanded to know what had happened to him. In the future, he said, he would prefer being put in bed and left alone to solve his own problems, rather than being subjected to medical guesswork, however well-intentioned it might be.

In 1906 Cayce was working with a Bowling Green physician, Dr. John Blackburn. He and Cayce had been approached by a teacher at the local business college who was concerned about a murder in his home town, in Canada. Could Cayce name the party who had killed the young girl in question?

Edgar had no idea whether he could deal with such a matter; certainly he had never done anything like it before. With his father, Dr. Blackburn and the teacher standing by he went into a trance. They read to him the name and address of the victim and asked him to name the killer. After a considerable pause, Edgar said that the murderer was the victim's sister. He gave the make, caliber and serial number on the pistol and told them the murder weapon was stuffed into a drain pipe in the basement.

Was this information true or false?

The teacher wired the statement to the authorities in his home town and waited for their reaction. It was not long in coming—in the person of the Chief of Police who had a warrant for the arrest of Edgar Cayce and the teacher —on suspicion of murder!

When the befuddled officer found out that the statement on which his charges were based was the result of a self-induced hypnotic trance, he threw a tantrum. But when Cayce went into another trance and described in detail the scene of the slaying and the girl who had allegedly committed the crime, the officer calmed down and hurried back to Canada. There, he led the sister to the basement and recovered the pistol. When he accused her of the crime and told her how he "knew"—the dumbfounded young woman stammered out the story of her guilt—a story that opened the prison doors for her.

Cayce, incidentally, had had enough of solving murder cases. He never again let himself become involved in such experiments.

When a disastrous fire left him heavily in debt, Cayce was subjected to one of the most gruelling experiences of his career to that point.

It involved a close personal friend, the wife of Dr. Thomas House, of Hopkinsville. Unable to diagnose his wife's ailment, Dr. House had called in a noted specialist, Dr. W. H. Haggard, of Nashville. The specialist decided that Mrs. House was suffering from an abdominal tumor which needed immediate surgery.

But Mrs. House insisted that her friend Cayce also be

asked for a "reading"—which he gave. It differed sharply with the diagnosis of Dr. Haggard and the other local medics who had been called in. Cayce's diagnosis was that the lady was pregnant and was also suffering from a locked bowel . . . and that no surgery was necessary.

Mrs. House demanded that she be treated in accordance with Edgar Cayce's instructions and, with considerable misgivings, Dr. House acquiesced. Sure enough, the locked bowel was present and responded to treatment. A few months later, Dr. Haggard's "tumor" arrived and was duly christened Thomas B. House, Jr.

This seems to have been the first occasion in the incredible saga of Edgar Cayce when he collided openly with professional medics and proved them wrong. Certainly it was not the last—fate had another test waiting for him and just around the corner, so to speak.

When the House baby was four months old, Mrs. House again sent for Edgar. The baby was having convulsions at the rate of one every twenty minutes. Dr. House and two other M.D.'s were there when Cayce arrived. They had agreed that the baby could not live more than a few hours at most. Edgar went at once to a bedroom where Dr. House described the case and took notes on what Cayce said in his trance.

Cayce prescribed belladonna—a poison—which shocked Dr. House and angered the other medics. One of them walked out. The other protested to Mrs. House. After he had finished she turned to her husband and said:

"This is the 'tumor' these same doctors diagnosed. The child will be dead in a few hours, according to their statements. Edgar Cayce told us the truth in the first place. I trust him now. Get the medicine he prescribed."

The belladonna was administered. In a matter of minutes the baby was relaxed and snoring peacefully. He outlived Edgar Cayce, in fact.

There had been considerable publicity regarding this strange man and his inexplicable "trance medicine" but at the time of the readings for the House baby Edgar had yet to meet the man who would single-handedly propel him into the national spotlight.

Edgar and his wife, then living in Gadsden, Alabama, had returned to Hopkinsville to spend the 1909 Christmas holidays with his parents. The Squire was less active due to his advancing years, but he still managed to find time to sing the praises of his remarkable son. Thus Edgar was probably not surprised when he arrived home to find that his father had arranged for him to meet with a new doctor in the town, Wesley Ketchum, a homeopath and a skeptic of the Cayce story.

Cayce's experiences with doctors, with a few exceptions, had not been happy. He was not unprepared for the thinly concealed challenge in Dr. Ketchum's greeting. The doctor said frankly that he, personally, needed a reading—to see if Cayce's diagnosis could define an ailment which the doctor said he had already confirmed for himself.

As a matter of fact, Edgar did not agree with the doctor. Edgar said, in his trance, that the doctor did *not* have appendicitis, merely a pinched nerve in the lower spine which could be relieved by an osteopath.

The doctor roared at this. He *knew* he had appendicitis and, just to prove Edgar a fraud, he would take the osteopathic treatment and *show* them. He marched across the street to the office of an osteopath, had a couple of misplaced vertebrae pushed back into place and got the surprise of his life: the "appendicitis" was gone!

He promptly began a study of the records which Dr. Blackburn and others had compiled during previous readings by Edgar Cayce, investigating many of the patients personally since they were within easy distance of Hopkinsville. It was upon this compilation of evidence that Ketchum based the report he made to the American Society of Clinical Research in the late summer of 1910 and which later inspired the article on Cayce in *The New York Times*.

Newsmen from many cities tracked Edgar down and pestered him for stories; scientists, including Dr. Hugo Munsterberg of Harvard, came to scoff and went away wondering.

For a while Edgar worked with a group of friends in Hopkinsville, giving readings twice each day for the hundreds who sent requests for help. It was no gold mine but it was a modest living. He went to Chicago as the guest of the Hearst papers; but, other than another burst of publicity, nothing lasting came of it.

Cayce realized that if he was to be more effective to those who sought his help he must have a permanent center for treatment and a place where the records of his work could be gathered and kept on a businesslike basis. In other words, he needed a hospital.

Among the thousands who came to him for health was Madison B. Wyrick, a plant superintendent for Western Union in Chicago, who was a diabetic. The treatment Cayce prescribed for him proved beneficial. It is interesting to note that it contained quantities of Jerusalem artichokes, a rich natural source of insulin.

Another patient who benefited from Edgar's readings was a New York businessman, Morton Blumenthal, whose chronic ear infection responded promptly to the treatment suggested.

They, and a few others of the thousands who had come to Cayce and found help, kept urging him to set up a hospital. At last Virginia Beach, then a rather rundown resort area, was chosen. A corporation was formed (The Association of National Investigators, a Virginia corporation, May 6, 1927) and Edgar Cayce, after years of drifting from pillar to post with his strange talent, had found a base of operations.

For a few years all went amazingly well. A hospital was built and doctors hired. Secretaries kept records of the thousands of readings that Cayce gave and made follow-up investigations on the results of the treatments.

The philosophy behind the treatments from the Cayce trance readings never varied: Treat the cause—not the effect. Help the entire system to become healthy and it will conquer the ailment.

This was brought into focus in a case which involved a young woman who was rapidly becoming bedfast with arthritis. Doctors were giving her the usual pain-killers while her condition steadily worsened. After she underwent the treatment prescribed by Cayce—a combination of special diets, massages and exercises, the improvement and eventual recovery quickly followed.

The stock market crash in 1929 was devastating to some of the key financial supporters of the institution at Virginia Beach. The hospital staggered bravely to a close as funds ran out. The patients were sent home.

216

In 1931 a new organization, the Association For Research and Enlightenment, was formed by a small group, largely residents of Virginia Beach or nearby communities. Edgar and his wife went to New York City where they were arrested, believe it or not!—on a charge of fortune telling. Edgar had given readings for two policewomen in plain clothes who had come to their hotel room pleading for assistance. The case was thrown out of court by a judge who had substantially more humane decency than Cayce's persecutors.

Perhaps the most lasting product at the Virginia Beach base was the carefully indexed records of the readings that Cayce gave through the years and the results of the treatments, gathered from the doctors who administered them and from the patients themselves. In those records are innumerable cases where Cayce, in trance, went back through the lifetimes of people whom he had never seen or heard of, and spelled out incidents in their lives which affected their health. He gave names and dates, in many cases incidents which had seemed so trivial at the time of their occurrence that those involved had almost forgotten them. These records contain what is probably the most astounding and documented evidence of clairvoyance ever compiled.

There is, for example, the case of a prescription for a product which Cayce called "Oil Of Smoke." The patient, in Louisville, could not locate such an item. Cayce went into trance and specified the drug store where it was available. Back came a telegram—the drug store did not have it. Another trance. Cayce told the patient to have the druggist look behind some other medicines on a certain shelf in the storage room. It was done, and three bottles of "Oil of Smoke," their labels yellowed with age, were found and put to good use.

Plagued by restricted income, medical opposition and advancing years, Mr. and Mrs. Cayce stayed on in Virginia Beach. They raised their family and kept their chins up, confident that they were doing the best they could with Edgar's strange gift. They had kept the records and they had kept the faith.

Edgar Cayce died January 3, 1945, at the age of sixty-seven, worn out by his years of exhaustive efforts on behalf of his fellow man.

What he did and how he did it are fully set forth in the records of his organization at Virginia Beach, Virginia. Through him more than twelve thousand persons were restored to health by carrying out the courses of treatment he prescribed, ofttimes in cases where conventional medicine had written off the patient as beyond improvement.

Although the record is voluminous and available to inspection, orthodox medicine has shown no interest.

Having ridiculed him in life, it ignores him in death.

AUTHOR'S NOTE: Cayce was curious as to the source and the nature of his strange power. He asked questions and the answers he dictated to his secretaries are set forth in considerable detail in Thomas Sugrue's excellent volume, *There Is A River,* published by Henry Holt and Co., 1942. It is based to a large extent on the author's personal discussions with Cayce and his associates and has become a standard reference on the subject.

The philosophical aspects of Cayce's life and work are

also to be found in *Many Mansions,* by Gina Cerminara, available in many libraries.

Cayce was not the first of the "sleeping doctors," for even in our own country he was preceded by Sleeping Lucy, whose story follows.

As far back as 1784, the Marquis de Puysegur reports that, when he hypnotized a young shepherd named Victor, the boy could diagnose ailments of persons near and far "and with most remarkable correctness."

And fortunate indeed is the student of such things who can locate a copy of *The Principles of Nature, Her Divine Revelations and A Voice To Mankind—by and Through Andrew Jackson Davis, The Poughkeepsie Seer and Clairvoyant, 1847.* Andrew Jackson Davis was a young man who prescribed medical treatments while in a trance. The book is his record, compiled in part by the two doctors who conducted the experiments. The book, like the trance doctor it concerns, is exceedingly rare.

39

Sleeping Lucy

Edgar Cayce was not the first of the unusual type of medical practitioners he represented; he was simply one who lived in an era where such matters were more adequately reported.

As a matter of record, Cayce was preceded a good many years in his field by an unusual lady known as "Sleeping Lucy"—Mrs. E. W. Raddin at the time of her death in North Cambridge, Massachusetts, shortly after the turn of the century. The papers gave her age as seventy-six and respectfully referred to her as "the well known Dr. Cooke, whose practice extends throughout New England." At the time of her demise, she had been practicing her unique form of medicine for fifty-three years.

Born Lucy Ainsworth in Calais, Vermont, she was about fourteen years old in 1833 when her strange gifts were first noticed. A neighbor, Nathan Barnes, had lost his thick gold watch, a family heirloom by which he set great store. He and his wife had searched for the timepiece until they were exhausted. Mrs. Barnes went to the Ainsworth homestead down the road to tearfully recount her husband's loss. Lucy was helping her mother with the dishes at the time and both she and her mother consoled the sobbing neighbor lady.

Mrs. Barnes went back home and Lucy went into the parlor to lie down. Although it was mid-morning, the girl felt strangely sleepy. A few moments later she was sound asleep.

She awakened shortly before noon to find her mother and her two brothers seated at the table in the dining room. Without any prefatory remarks she blurted out: "Mr. Barnes' watch fell out of his pocket while he was sleeping in the hammock under the pear tree! Tell him he will find it there—in the grass under the hammock!"

He *did* find it there, just as Lucy Ainsworth had assured her family. News of this little event spread quickly through the small community, of course. There were the usual pat explanations and the scoffers; but, when Lucy had found similar objects for others by simply going to sleep and "dreaming" where the missing objects were located, it became a community by-word to "Let Sleeping Lucy find it" whenever anything was lost. From the description of her actions it is quite clear that she went into a trance for her "nap" and, after the first few times, she could not recall in her waking state what had been "seen" while she was unconscious. Her instructions were given verbally while she was stretched on the couch, eyes closed, pulse slowed and breathing slow and heavy.

Lucy married a neighboring farmer named Cooke, who, with her brothers Luther and George, directed her activities.

Like Edgar Cayce, Lucy had only a modest education and no training at all in medicine. Yet, as her unusual talents developed, she began to prescribe, diagnose and even

221

to set bones while in her trance state. The patients who came to her from far and near were enthusiastic in their descriptions of her abilities. Those with broken bones and dislocations stated that "Sleeping Lucy," now becoming known as Doctor Cooke, performed her deeds with little or no pain, even though no anaesthetic was used.

A typical case was that of a boy of eleven, whose right leg was broken above the ankle and whose right arm was dislocated at the shoulder, the result of a fall from a tree. The boy had been treated in his home town of Montpelier by local medics, but the pain was so great that he could not sleep. He ran a high fever. In spite of the agony of the journey, the youngster's parents put him in a wagon and drove him to "Sleeping Lucy's" farm, then out on East Montpelier Road.

The child was placed on his back on a couch across the room from the strange "Doctor," who promptly went into a trance. First, she described in detail what was wrong with him. Then she slowly gave orders for a prescription to be used to reduce his fever. Then, still in the trance, she arose slowly and stiffly from her couch and crossed the room to where the feverish, pain-wrecked child was lying.

Lucy's fingers touched him lightly on the upper arm and then traced their way ever so gently to that swollen leg, near the ankle. She seemed to find the break as though she had X-ray vision, for without hesitation she grasped the inflamed limb above and below the break, tugged gently with a slight twist, and ordered that it be bound with a stiff cloth. A moment later she deftly put the arm back in its socket, evidently without strain or pain. The boy never even whimpered. He just sighed deeply and dropped off into the first real sleep he had had for a week

—and his parents later told Lucy that the child slept all the way home in spite of the jolting wagon bed.

When she entered the trance state, Lucy became a forceful, authoritative medical practitioner. She ofttimes found herself at odds with more conventional doctors who had previously diagnosed some of the same cases, but this was a matter of small concern to this simple country-girl-turned-medic. She made her diagnosis in detail, prescribed treatments which were sometimes years ahead of her time and became one of the best known and most successful doctors of her era.

After the death of her first husband, Lucy married Everett W. Raddin of Danvers, Massachusetts, in 1898. Mr. Raddin took up the task of inducing the trance, which became increasingly difficult as she grew older, and the burdens of treating the number of patients increased steadily. In order to compound some of her prescriptions, she had to establish her own drug laboratory where pharmacists could quickly provide the chemicals she specified.

For twenty years she practiced in Montpelier, Vermont, and for twelve years in Boston. In 1900, she was living in North Cambridge, her home often marked by a line of waiting patients who had come from all parts of New England seeking the help of this strange woman, whom science could neither explain nor duplicate.

She, like Edgar Cayce who came after her, seemed to draw upon some source which she did not understand and which she did not control. But whatever it was, and wherever it was, "Sleeping Lucy" used it for fifty-three years for the benefit of those who came to her in search of help.

40

The Return Of Tom Harris

William Briggs and Tom Harris had been friends for many years and it was only natural that they shared many confidences. They fought side by side in the Revolutionary War; they farmed together in Queen Anne's County, Maryland. They were, in short, lifelong buddies.

In the early fall of 1790, Tom Harris and his brother James were stacking sheaves of wheat in Tom's barnyard when Tom suddenly staggered and slumped to the ground. A few hours later Tom Harris had died without regaining consciousness.

Tom had left a will which instructed the court to sell his property and divide the proceeds equally among his four illegitimate children. The will named his younger brother James as executor and early in 1791 James undertook to carry out the terms of the document. He found a buyer for the farm, which was a good one, but he also found something else. Under the condition by which Tom held the property, he could dispose of it only to his heirs, which meant that his illegitimate children, having no legal status, could not receive the proceeds.

James recognized the chance to take over when he saw it. He petitioned the court to award him the monies received from settling his brother's estate, leaving Tom's illegitimate children with nothing.

Briggs had purchased Tom's favorite horse shortly after his friend's death. According to subsequent court testimony, this was the animal he was riding on a bright sunshiny morning in March of 1791 jogging along on his way to a neighboring town.

The narrow road led past the burying ground where Tom Harris had been laid to rest seven months before. Briggs told the court that he was speculating on what his friend would have said or done could he have known how his brother, James, was seeking to deprive Tom's children of their share of the estate. Suddenly Tom's horse stopped, stared into the graveyard and then neighed loudly as it always had done when it spied its master. Briggs said that goose pimples stood out on his arms as he looked into the graveyard; for there, walking slowly toward him in the bright sunshine was his long-time friend, the late Tom Harris. The specter approached the rail fence between them and then vanished in the twinkling of an eye.

"It was Tom, all right!" Briggs told the court. "With that limp he got when a Tory shot him in the leg at Monmouth. He had on the same suit he was buried in. His eyes were wide open and staring. His grey hair was all mussed up like he had just yanked his hat off. He walked right up close to the fence, sort of stiff-armed and awkward. Then he turned right and disappeared all at once."

Briggs testified that his old friend in spectral form appeared to him so many times in the ensuing months that he was terrified by the experiences. Tom would awaken

Briggs in the middle of the night by striking him. He pestered Briggs about twice each week until August and then he failed to appear for several weeks, and Briggs was encouraged to believe that the awesome visitations had ended.

However, this was not the case.

One October morning, shortly before sunrise, Briggs and his hired man, a fellow named Bailey, were driving some cows into a field behind the barn when Briggs was startled to see Tom Harris walking straight toward them along a fence between the lane and a garden. When he was about twenty feet away Harris suddenly vanished. Briggs had stopped in his tracks when he first noticed the apparition and when it was gone he found his companion gazing at him in wonderment.

Had Bailey seen Tom Harris? Bailey had not. Then Briggs began to wonder if *he* had seen his old friend, or if, as he was beginning to suspect, he was losing his sanity.

Two hours afterward, Briggs later testified, Harris appeared again, about twenty feet from where Briggs and Bailey were working along a stone fence. The specter beckoned to him, said Briggs, and he moved to within a few feet of it.

"Why don't you go to your brother?" Briggs asked.

"Don't ask questions," said the strange visitor in a voice that was scarcely more than a whisper.

"But there is trouble about your will. Why don't you go to your brother—I can't do anything about it."

"Go to my brother James and ask him if he remembers the conversation we had on the east side of the wheat shocks on the day that I was stricken. I told him then that I wanted all my property kept together until my children were of age. I do not want it sold now. After I made that first will, I realized that it was a mistake. I wanted the children to have the income from the property while they were minors. When they became of age I wanted it sold and the proceeds divided among them, so I made another will. James knows about it. Ask him. You will see me again."

Then he vanished, said Briggs.

In accordance with the instructions from his late friend, Briggs confronted James Harris with the message that he had been requested to deliver. James declared that he did not believe that Briggs had seen his deceased brother and flatly denied that there had been any conversation beside the wheat shocks.

"Very well, then," said Briggs, "let me refresh your memory."

Briggs told the court later that, as he related to James the details of the conversation between himself and the phantom, James blanched and stood speechless for a moment. Then he replied:

"You have talked to Tom, all right! There was nobody else who could have known what was said that afternoon. We were the only ones who knew about it!" James began to shake as though he were having a hard chill, said Briggs. After a few minutes he turned to Briggs and said: "I'll do what Tom told me to do! I'll see that his kids get the property!"

For the fourth time that day in October of 1791, according to the testimony of William Briggs, he found himself in the company of the late Tom Harris. This final visitation occurred as he was trudging along the road near his home, Briggs testified, and the gist of it was that Harris said he hoped that his brother would keep his word so that he, Tom Harris, could rest at last, knowing that his children were not being cheated.

John Bailey, the hired man who had been with Briggs that day, testified that he had not actually seen Tom Harris as Briggs seemed to do, but that he had heard a voice other than that of Briggs and that the voice and Briggs were unquestionably carrying on a conversation, the details of which he did not know.

James Harris died suddenly without having carried out the terms of his brother's second will, which Briggs said he promised to do. The widow of James Harris denounced the whole story as a fraud designed to cheat her of her husband's estate in favor of four illegitimate children.

The case went to court as The State of Maryland versus Mary Harris, Administratrix of the estate of James Harris. The court accepted the testimony of William Briggs, including his alleged experiences with the ghost of his old friend Tom Harris.

The attorney for Mrs. James Harris ridiculed and criticized Briggs and sought to make him appear to be lying about his conversation with the phantom. But Briggs steadfastly withstood the scornful attack and, according to a pamphlet written by a member of the Baltimore council who was present, Briggs convinced his auditors that he had told the truth, bizarre as it was.

41

Long Range
Telepathy

In October, 1937, Sir Hubert Wilkins
was preparing to set out on another of his epic struggles
with the Arctic. This one was in search of a Russian flier
who had vanished in an attempt to fly over the Arctic to
this country by way of Alaska. This was to be Sir Hubert's
eleventh trip into the frozen polar wilderness; trips which
had won for him the admiration of such men as Ellsworth,
Byrd and other great explorers.

Wilkins had long been interested in telepathic com-
munication and, when his personal friend, Harold Sherman, suggested some experiments in that field during the
trip, Sir Hubert was immediately interested.

It was agreed that Sherman would sit still for three
thirty-minute periods per week, eleven-thirty till midnight
EST, on Mondays, Tuesdays and Thursdays as soon as
Wilkins left on his trip. In his turn, the explorer was to
try to project his thoughts on what was happening to
himself during those same periods.

Two precautions were taken to keep the records straight:
Sherman was to mail to Dr. Gardner Murphy, the head of

the Department of Parapsychology at Columbia University, the impressions he was receiving on the nights they were received. The other precaution was for Reginald Iverson, chief operator of *The New York Times* short wave station, to report to Wilkins on the progress, if any, of the experiments.

In addition to Dr. Murphy receiving the reports from Sherman, Dr. A. E. Strath-Gordon and Dr. Henry Hardwicke, both personal friends of Sir Hubert at the City Club in New York, were to act as observers on his behalf during the sittings.

The short wave radio communications with Wilkins and his party were badly hampered by static due to the magnetic storms which raged throughout most of the trip. Actually, Iverson got through to them only thirteen times. And Sherman? Let the famed explorer tell it:

"Many nights I was unable to keep my appointments with Sherman, but he and I were both surprised to note that his mental impressions of what had happened to me maintained a high percentage of accuracy. It soon became evident that Sherman, in some manner not understood by us, was picking up quite a number of strong thought-forms—strong thoughts emitted by me during the day—and some of which I had at times tried to pass on to him at our regularly scheduled periods."

Sir Hubert writes that since he was sometimes unable to keep his "appointments" with Sherman, he decided to "project" the thoughts whenever it was most convenient for him, and this was the pattern he followed.

The missing Russian flier, Levanevsky, was never found, although Sir Hubert flew more than forty thousand miles in miserable and dangerous weather.

The famed explorer kept a careful and complete diary of each day's activities. Several thousand miles away, Sherman's impressions of those activities were being written down and filed regularly with Columbia University and with the two doctors who represented Wilkins as observers.

Said Sir Hubert in his account of the experiment:

"And when we finally were able to compare notes, what did we find? An amazing number of impressions recorded by Sherman of expedition happenings, as well as personal experiences, thoughts and reactions of mine. Too many of them approximately correct and synchronized with the very day of the occurrences to have been guesswork."

On the night of March 14, 1938, Sherman wrote: "Believe you discovered crack of framework in tail of fuselage which needed repair. (Correct, according to Sir Hubert's daily records.) Seem to see you manipulating hand pump of some sort in flight. One engine is emitting spouts of black smoke—uneven, choked sound—as though carburetor trouble."

Sir Hubert said of this last portion of the report: "During the day in changing over from one gas tank to another I was late in switching and had to pump furiously with the engine sputtering and coughing to keep them going. It lasted only a few minutes but it occupied my mind much of the day."

Continuing, Sherman's report said that Wilkins was watching dangerous rime ice form on the wings of the plane which seemed to be at location of 86-115. This also was in accordance with the facts except that Sherman had missed the exact location by 45 miles from a point 3,000 miles away.

Small wonder that Sir Hubert was amazed at some of

the details in the reports that Sherman was receiving mentally at that great distance. Among other things, the famed explorer found himself having to borrow a dress suit to attend a hastily-arranged function in Regina, Saskatchewan, when his plane was forced down there in a snowstorm on November 11, 1937. The borrowed suit was designed for a much smaller man but Wilkins struggled into it and went to the ball, in company with Army officers, Mounted Police and their ladies.

"You are in company with men in military attire—some women—evening dress—social occasion—important people present—much conversation. You appear to be in evening dress yourself!" Sherman was viewing the scene from New York City, sitting in his armchair beside the two observers.

On December 7th, 1937, Sherman wrote: "I seem to see a crackling fire shining out of the darkness—I get a definite fire impression as though a house were burning. You can see it from your location on the ice. Quite a crowd gathered around it. Many people running or hurrying toward the flames. Bitter cold. Stiff wind blowing."

True or false?

Sir Hubert said: "As I was actually seeing that fire in the Far North (it was an Eskimo's shack at Point Barrow) Sherman, tuned in on my mind, was seeing the *same* fire in his consciousness, while seated in his study in New York!"

On the night of December 9th, just 48 hours after the fire scene, Sherman wrote in his report: "I see you, connection school, standing front of blackboard—chalk in hand. You give short talk, illustrating remarks."

On the night of December 9th, at the time Sherman was writing this, Sir Hubert's diary shows that he was speaking to the school children in Point Barrow and illustrating his remarks with chalk drawings.

There were many other instances wherein the reports Sherman filed in New York closely matched the events the famous explorer was experiencing and recording in his diary in the Arctic. In fairness it must be admitted that there were times when Sherman received nothing and times when what he wrote down was incorrect or only partially correct.

That he should have received anything is remarkable.

That he received so many reports which matched those of the sender is astounding and inexplicable.

In summation, Sir Hubert Wilkins wrote:

"We may not have proved that telepathy between two people at some distance apart is beyond doubt, and possible by arrangement, but I was personally pleased to have been engaged in the experiment, and feel that we *have* proved that the subject is entirely worthy of much further attention."

Recommended additional reading: *Thoughts Through Space,* by H. T. Sherman.

42

Stevenson
Dreamed A Classic

Robert Louis Stevenson made no secret of his uncanny ability to dream at will of the plots for his stories. He often spoke of this peculiar capacity and in particular of how he had called upon it at a crucial moment in his career.

Stevenson, like most writers, had a period during which his name alone did not assure acceptance of material. It was during this time that he conceived a short story which he titled "The Traveling Companion," based on the theme of a dual personality—one good, one evil. He completed the story and sent it in to an editor, who promptly rejected it with a note saying, "This is an ingenious piece of work but your plot is very weak."

The writer read the story again and recognized the truth of the criticism. He also recognized his own inability to improve on the plot and thus he was stalemated for weeks while the unsalable story gathered dust instead of dollars. Then he recalled his ability to call forth plots in his dreams, where he would simply stand aside as a spectator and watch a story as it unfolded, without knowing how it would end. Could this extraordinary talent solve his predicament?

Just before he went to sleep that night, Stevenson reread his rejected short story. In the subsequent dream he witnessed the development of a strange drama which he promptly set down in writing when he awakened. In his fantastic dream he had seen the dual-personality theme of his short story expanded into a fantastic plot which became world-famous—the story of Dr. Jekyll and Mr. Hyde.

43

The Man Who Was
Hanged Three Times

Someone had stolen a small writing desk which, when last seen, had contained a bag of gold and silver coins. The year was 1803 and the actual loss in the theft did not exceed two hundred dollars, but the thief, or thieves, had dealt such grievous wounds to a police constable who happened upon them that he later died of the injuries.

The police of Sydney, Australia, went after the guilty party or parties with a vengeance and when they finally caught up with Joseph Samuels, a man of ill-repute, and found some of the missing coins in his pockets, they promptly charged him with the murder of the constable.

It mattered not that he produced witnesses who corroborated his story of having won the coins in a gambling den. It availed him nothing that numerous other witnesses testified that he had been in a drunken stupor at the time of the robbery and miles from where it took place.

Joseph Samuels was induced to confess to the robbery and the court promptly found him guilty of the murder on circumstantial evidence. He had stuck his own neck in the noose by confessing to the robbery, which had set the stage for the slaying. He was sentenced to be hanged in September of 1803.

An accomplice, Isaac Simmonds, was still in custody but police had been unable to trick him into confessing anything and, with the grim spectacle of Samuels before him, his reluctance was quite understandable. As a maneuver which might shock him into talking, the Provost Marshal ordered Simmonds brought to witness the hanging of his partner in crime.

As he stood in the death cart beside the gallows on the morning set for his execution, Samuels delivered a little speech to the assemblage. He reiterated his confession that he had indeed helped to steal the desk and he reiterated his denial of having taken part in the murder of the constable. In fact, said Samuels calmly and without bitterness, the real murderer was there in the crowd, brought there under police guard to witness the execution of Samuels for a crime which had been committed by Isaac Simmonds.

At the mention of his name, Simmonds began to shout, trying to drown the words of the man in the death cart. But Samuels continued to describe what had happened and to weave the knot of suspicion around the neck of the bellowing, red-faced Simmonds.

Guards had already placed the noose around Samuels' neck before he began his speech. As he talked, a murmur ran through the crowd. It grew to a shout—a roar that Simmonds be tried and Samuels released. As the spectators surged forward, evidently intent on releasing the doomed man, a guard jabbed the cart horses and the vehicle was jerked from under Samuels. He dangled for a second and then the rope broke, dropping him to the earth on his face.

The guards formed a hollow square to hold back the mob until the hangman could put up a new rope. Samuels, only half-conscious from his first ordeal, was again placed in the cart, this time seated on a barrel since he was unable to stand. The Provost Marshal gave the order and the cart was again yanked from beneath the ill-fated fellow. As the crowd watched in horror, the rope began to unwind, strand by strand, until Samuels' feet dragged on the ground, giving him just enough support to keep him from suffocating.

The crowd let out a roar.

"Cut him down! Cut him down! It is God's will!"

But the Provost Marshal did not credit the bungling with any divine origin. He ordered the soldiers to put still another rope around Samuels' neck and, for the third time, the condemned man was subjected to a violent drop at the end of the rope. This time it broke, just above his head.

A soldier loosened the noose so that Samuels could breathe if he still had the will to do so. The unnerved Provost Marshal jumped on his horse and rode full tilt to the Governor's office to report on this incredible series of accidents.

The Governor promptly issued a reprieve, but it took Samuels some time to realize what was taking place. A contemporary account says that he was "somewhat confused and addled in his mind and could not at first accept the merciful tidings which were brought to him."

After the principal character in this unique drama had been led from the scene, the suspicious Provost Marshal proceeded to conduct an investigation of the ropes which had played such a surprising part. Had they been tampered with?

Examination showed that the ropes had *not* been sabotaged. The last rope, which had snapped like a piece of twine, was a new one and was tested with a twenty-eight-stone weight (about three hundred and ninety pounds) in drop after drop. Even when two of the strands had been cut, the one remaining held the full weight—yet it had broken through all three strands when Samuels had dangled from its noose.

The records of the case show that Isaac Simmonds was subsequently tried and hanged for the murder of the constable.

And what of Joseph Samuels, who had been hanged thrice in one morning and lived to tell about it?

I regret to report that Joseph soon returned to his evil companions and their dubious enterprises. Robbery, drunkenness, knifing and mutiny were among his activities. In jail again, he found that he stood a good chance of facing a newer and stronger rope, for he had become a public nuisance.

When last heard of, Joseph Samuels and a group of fellow convicts managed to steal a ship's boat in which they escaped from Newcastle. The man who survived three trips to the gallows had tempted fate once too often, for neither he nor his companions were ever seen again.

44

Another Who Skipped The Rope

Joseph Samuels wasn't the only condemned man who skipped the hanging rope. When John Lee was convicted of the particularly brutal murder of an old woman, he was sentenced to be hanged at Exeter, England.

On the gray, cold and windy morning of February 23, 1895, Lee was led to the scaffold. About a hundred witnesses were present, some in official capacities and others out of morbid curiosity. The hangman was a veteran who had carefully checked the components of his lethal machinery. The rope had been stretched and oiled, the trapdoor hinges greased, the trigger that released the trap door carefully gone over and found in good working order.

Lee's thin prison garments were whipped about him by the wind as he stumbled up the steps. He muttered that he was cold, but his guards ignored the complaint; for certainly he would not be cold very long. John Lee shuffled into place on the trap door and his hands were tightly tied behind his back. Did he have anything to say? He shook his head. The way his teeth were chattering it is doubtful whether he *could* have said anything. It seemed that all involved, including the man with the noose around his neck, were eager to have done with this grisly business.

The signal was given and the hangman pulled the trigger that held up the trap door.

Nothing happened.

Lee stood there helplessly, his masked head bowed, waiting for the drop. The hangman scurried under the scaffold to search for the trouble. He found that the bolt had slid into its recess as planned, but the trap door with Lee's weight on it never moved.

One of the officials took Lee by the arm and had him step back while the hangman reset the door and tested it. When the bolt was pulled, the door dropped swiftly.

The condemned man was moved back into place. Again the bolt was pulled. Again the trap door refused to budge.

A ripple of comment ran through the shivering crowd of spectators. The officials felt that something had to be done quickly; so the warden himself stood on the trap door, hanging to the hands of two guards on the platform on either side of him. The trap door shot from under him and left him dangling.

In the meantime, John Lee had been led back to his cell, puzzled by all this delay. He could not understand what was happening since he could not see anything. At the warden's signal he was brought back to the scaffold; and for a third—and still a fourth—time the bolt was pulled but the trap door never moved.

By this time the warden was sweating profusely, as were the hangman and the guards. They admitted that they felt dreadfully uneasy—as though they were trying to defy a power that they could only sense without seeing. Without

John Lee on the trap door the thing worked perfectly; but when he took his place there it defied gravity. Why?

The sheriff decided to call a halt to the execution while he submitted the report to his superiors. It was referred to the Home Secretary. It was eventually debated in Parliament. Finally, the death sentence of John Lee was commuted to life imprisonment. But that, too, was quietly reduced to only a few years' imprisonment and John Lee soon walked out of the prison a free man.

Although lengthy investigation of the scaffold was made immediately, they found nothing to explain the strange case of the trap door that refused to fall when John Lee's neck was in the noose.

Perhaps Lee himself had the answer when he told newspapermen years later: "I have always had a feeling that I had help from some Power greater than gravity!"

45

Will Purvis, Who
Would Not Die

It was a blazing August day in 1893 when the Mississippi jury left the court room to decide the fate of twenty-one-year-old Will Purvis, accused of killing a fellow farmer after a quarrel. Will admitted the quarrel but denied the killing; but he had no evidence to support his claim. As he sat, head in hands, the only sound in the courtroom was the droning of flies and the nervous shuffling of feet. The general feeling was that the jury would not be out very long—and it wasn't.

". . . guilty as charged," said the foreman.

". . . hanged by the neck until dead!" said the judge.

It was February 7, 1894, when they led Will Purvis to the gallows where he was to square his debt to society, as legalized murder is described. A crowd of hundreds had gathered to witness the gruesome spectacle. Many of them felt that Purvis was innocent just because they had known him all his life and knew that he was simply not a killer. But there was nothing they could do now. The black hood was dropped over his head, the noose adjusted behind his ear and, when the sheriff gave the signal, the trap was sprung.

Will plunged through the hole in the gallows floor but instead of breaking his neck he managed to stagger to his feet—unhurt! A most remarkable thing had happened. The thick rope had uncoiled at the noose!

In accordance with the orders of the court—to hang him until dead—the deputies led Purvis back up to the scaffold and the hangman re-knotted the noose. But by this time the crowd was angry. As far as they were concerned, they had seen a miracle; they had seen Will Purvis get a reprieve from the Highest Court of all. They began to chant. The chant quickly grew to a roar. The sheriff realized that, unless he did something quickly he could lose control of the situation, so he personally yanked off the hood and led Will back to his cell.

The doomed man's attorneys filed three appeals to the State Supreme Court and all three were turned down. Miracle or no miracle, Will Purvis had been tried and found guilty and sentenced to hang—and hang he must, on December 12, 1895.

That was only the court's idea. Will's friends and neighbors had another idea. They broke into the jail and carried him away one stormy night when the deputy sheriff happened to be looking the other way. Furthermore, Will was hidden for a year among his benefactors, a year that brought a new governor to office. That worthy commuted Will's sentence to life imprisonment when the fugitive surrendered to the law.

By this time the case had caught the fancy of the entire state and thousands of letters poured in on the Mississippi State House demanding a full pardon for this man whose life had been spared in such strange fashion. In due time the Governor yielded to public pressure and Will Purvis walked out of the state penitentiary a free man.

Was he really innocent of the murder for which he had almost paid with his life? Will contended that he was, but there the matter rested for twenty-two years; until a man named Joe Beard lay dying in 1920. Beard wanted to get something off his mind, he said; and he called for witnesses, who took down his words as he told how he had killed the man for whose slaying Will Purvis had been convicted and sentenced.

46

The Ghost That Went To Court

Jim Chaffin was known as a pinch-penny, eccentric farmer who lived in Davis County, North Carolina. He was considered well-to-do but it would have been difficult to guess from his appearance, since he wore cheap clothing and topped it off with a shabby old overcoat most of the year.

He was happily married and the father of four sons: John, James, Marshall and Abner, in that order. He was fond of all of them but there was no misunderstanding in the family; Marshall was his father's favorite. This he set down in writing on November 16, 1905, when he made his will, appointing Marshall sole recipient of his estate and naming Marshall executor.

The document was witnessed and shown to the entire family. His wife and his other three sons were unpleasantly surprised by this turn of events and for a time there was some friction in the family. But finally they accepted it as just another eccentricity in the life of a man who had been noted for his unpredictable actions and the family settled down to its normal routine.

The aging man fell down some stairs and suffered internal injuries to which he succumbed on September

7, 1921. When Marshall filed the will for probate seventeen days later, the rest of the family did not contest; for they knew it was a valid document. After due process, the court turned over all the property of James L. Chaffin to his son and heir, Marshall.

For a year or so there was little visiting between the rest of the family and Marshall. They were still angry over the unequal distribution of the estate and even the mother found it difficult to maintain the same feeling towards her third son that she had for the others. But gradually the coolness that had flared after the court decree subsided and once again the Chaffin family managed to renew friendly relations among its members.

One night in June of 1925, almost four years after his father's death, James Chaffin (the second son) had a nightmare that left him soaked with perspiration. He dreamed that his father had appeared beside his bed, wearing that same moth-eaten old overcoat that had been his constant companion for so many years. The father slowly pulled back the overcoat and pointed to the inside pocket on the left breast. Again and again he pointed to the pocket. Then the dream faded and James awoke, badly shaken by the realistic quality of the nightmare.

He told his wife about it and sought to dismiss it as just another bad dream, but the experience made such an imprint on his mind that it bothered him all morning. Perhaps his mother would understand if he told her about it. At least it would help get it off his mind. James rode to his mother's house and recounted his weird nocturnal experience to her.

Mrs. Chaffin remembered the coat, of course, and she also recalled that she had given it to the eldest son, John, shortly after the father's death. Since John lived about twenty miles away, James and his mother decided to wait and make the trip on the following Monday.

They found that John was away from home but his wife recalled that John had worn the old coat only a couple of times and had then hung it in an upstairs attic, since he had considered it too big and too bedraggled for him.

The little group got the mossy old garment from its storage place and spread it on the bed. Was there any meaning to the dream or was it simply an experience which had sent them on a wild goose chase? They would know in a moment.

James found a pocket on the inside over the left breast . . . found it . . . and found it sewn shut! His mother took one look at the clumsy stitches and said: "Your father did that sewing—just look at the patchwork in those stitches!" With a pocketknife James slit the pocket open and probed inside it with his fingers. They brought out a tightly rolled slip of paper tied with a bit of string. Its edges were worn and tattered; evidently it had been in that pocket for years.

On it was written: "Read the 27th Chapter of Genesis in my daddy's old Bible." Those present recognized the handwriting as that of the elder James Chaffin. They knew that his father, Nathan, had been a circuit-riding clergyman whose Bible had been his constant companion most of his life and he had given it to James as a keepsake. It was in such bad shape that the elder James Chaffin had kept it wrapped in newspapers in an upstairs bedroom of his home. None of the family had seen the Bible for years and, in fact, only the mother knew exactly where she had last seen it.

This dramatic turn of events brought to those present the realization that the dream might have some substance to it, after all. Especially since the Bible Chapter recommended by the scrap of paper told the story of how the younger brother, Jacob, had won his father's favor and supplanted the elder brother, Esau, in his father's blessing. It was a parallel reminiscent of the recent events in the Chaffin family.

Somewhat shaken by the way things were developing, James decided that it would be a very good idea to have some witnesses other than family members before proceeding further. Accordingly, he induced a neighbor, Mr. Blackwelder, and Blackwelder's daughter to accompany the family group to his mother's house for the next step of this unusual project.

The elder Mrs. Chaffin recalled that the old Bible had been in bad condition when her late husband had stored it away for safekeeping shortly before his death. She quickly located it in a drawer full of keepsakes and, as James started to lift it out, the brittle wrappings tore and the Bible fell to the floor in three segments. Blackwelder picked up the section that contained the Book of Genesis. When he tried to open it at the 27th Chapter, he found that two pages had been folded tightly to form a sort of pocket. In that pocket was a slip of paper, evidently quite old and unmistakably written by the late James Chaffin. It read:

"After reading the 27th Chapter of Genesis, I, James L. Chaffin, do make my last will and testament, and here it is. I want, after giving my body a decent burial, my little property to be equally divided between my four children, if they are living at my death, both personal and real estate divided equal, if not living with share going to their children. And if she is living you all must take care of your mammy. Now this is my last will and testament. Witness my hand and seal.

James L. Chaffin

This January 16th, 1919"

The coolness between Marshall Chaffin, who had in-inherited everything under the 1905 will, and the rest of the family was clearly indicated by the manner in which the case was reopened.

Although the second will was unattested it was accepted as legal because it was so unmistakably the writing of James L. Chaffin that it was not even questioned. When the son who had found it presented it to the court for probate with a request that the first will be set aside, the action was promptly instituted. Since Marshall had died in the meantime, his young son was named defendant and Marshall's widow decided to appear in court as the child's next friend. But when she was shown the second will she conceded that it was indeed the elder Chaffin's handwriting and a valid instrument.

During the court proceedings, James related the strange dream which had directed him to the document. Although it was suggested that he had heard his father mention such a will at some time or other, the family all agreed that the father had never at any time even hinted at such a paper, but some reason of his own had taken pains to refer only to the 1905 document. Well, then, had James forged the second paper? Handwriting experts unanimously agreed that the wills were written by the same hand.

The court of Davis County, North Carolina, accepted the second will, to which James Chaffin had been directed by his strange dream. It remains on the records as a case in which the instructions of a ghost have been carried out by a court of law.

47

The Remarkable Dream Of
Sir E. A. Wallis Budge

For many years archeologists had been baffled by the steadily mounting supply of cuneiform tablets the field expeditions were sending in, tablets which carried messages in the long-forgotten Assyrian and Akkadian languages. It remained for a brilliant, impoverished youngster from Cornwall to unravel these tablets, a feat which the established scientists couldn't accomplish—but even our hero had to have help, and he got it from a dream.

In the annals of science the name of Sir E. A. Wallis Budge ranks among the foremost in his field and his *Hieroglyphical Dictionary*, published in 1920, is one of his many remarkable achievements still used by scholars.

Born in Cornwall in 1857, his chances of securing a degree at college were as poor as his parents. From childhood, young Budge showed a strong leaning toward oriental languages. By the time he was twenty-one he had become such an avid student in his chosen field that he had aroused the interest of the former Prime Minister, William Gladstone, himself a master of the classical languages. It was Gladstone who quietly arranged for this intense young

251

man to attend Christ's College at Cambridge in the category of a "non-collegiate student"—a nice way of separating him from the students who were financing themselves.

In the meanwhile, from the ruins of Nineveh and the other long-dead centers of civilization in Mesopotamia, the scholars had been deluged with undecipherable baked-mud tablets covered with cuneiform inscriptions. Made with tiny wedges dabbed into the soft mud, the writings resembled bird tracks and as far as the scholars were concerned in 1878 they might as well have been bird tracks. The Akkadian writing resembled Assyrian in many ways, and the scholars had learned to translate Assyrian to English. But Akkadian only *resembled* Assyrian, it differed in many bewildering and heartbreaking ways from its successor.

A series of clay tablets found in the debris of Nineveh on the site of King Ashurbanipal's palace appeared to be the key to the riddle, for they seemed to bridge the linguistic gap. Again it was a deceptive resemblance; a great deal of tedious translation resulted in nothing more than the disclosure of a single sentence and even that was debatable.

The young charity student, Budge, was invited about this time to participate in a competition involving oriental languages. The winner was to receive a fellowship (then called an "exhibition") and the competition was to be conducted by Oxford's noted Professor Sayce, then one of the greatest living authorities on ancient languages. The eminent scholar required the contestants to answer four questions at considerable length, asking them to remain at their task until their papers were completed.

For young Budge it was the chance of a lifetime. If he could win it, he could continue and expand his education at Cambridge and his prospects of becoming a success in his chosen field would be enhanced.

The opportunity was there, almost within his grasp, but the excited scholar found himself thwarted by a mind that had seemingly gone blank just when he needed it to function at its best. It was the night before the crucial examination but, in spite of frenzied attempts to bolster his learning with some last-minute study, Budge knew only frustration.

It was in this state of mind that he flung himself into bed, so exhausted mentally and physically that he went right to sleep and began to dream.

He seemed to be in a rather unusual room, taking his examination; in fact, he had the impression that he was in a shed of some sort. This was odd; for competitions were not held in sheds, even sheds with murky skylights such as this one had. As he pondered this peculiar aspect of his situation, a tutor entered the shed-like structure and pulled from his breast pocket an envelope from which he extracted several long slips of green paper. He instructed Budge to give complete answers to the questions on the green paper and to translate the texts. Then the tutor locked Budge in the room and left him to his problem. In the dream, the young man recognized questions as matters which he could answer easily—but when he turned to the material to be translated it was in the deceptive multi-lingual cuneiform Assyrian characters and in the equally difficult Akkadian language. Budge had a feeling of fright —of fear that he had failed—and then he woke up.

A short time later when he again went to sleep he repeated that same dream—and then experienced it still a third time. Soaked with sweat, he awakened and looked at the clock. He had been in bed about two hours all told, for it was only a few minutes past two in the morning.

The memory of those texts to be translated was fresh in his mind. The student recalled that they were included in Rawlinson's *Cuneiform Inscriptions of Western Asia* and, after a moment's search, he located them there. Budge hastily got into his clothes and spent the rest of the early morning hours reading and re-reading the ancient texts he had seen over and over in his series of dreams.

The hour set for the examination was nine o'clock and Budge was there. But the examination hall was already filled and an attendant told him to go to another room at the other end of the hall near the service quarters. It was a room which he had never seen before—except in his dreams. There was the shed-like roof with the dingy skylight, the scarred table, the single chair identical to the details of his dreams a few hours before.

As Budge stood there contemplating this remarkable state of affairs, the door opened and there entered the tutor who had also been in the dreams. The tutor pulled from his breast pocket the anticipated envelope and took from it four long slips of green paper. Noticing that Budge was staring at the green slip which he had given him, the tutor explained that Professor Sayce used green paper when writing cuneiform because it seemed to cause less eyestrain for him. With that the tutor stepped out, closed the door and left young Budge sitting there speechless with disbelief. On the green slip of paper were the questions and the cuneiform texts identical to those he had seen in his strange dreams a few hours before!

With such a briefing it is small wonder that Budge romped through the competition, and went on to become one of the all-time greats in the field he had chosen for his life's work. He is best known for his monumental translation of the Egyptian *Book of the Dead* and he was unquestionably the best Semitic scholar of his generation. It is probable that his most important contributions to Egyptology lay in his deciphering the hieratic papyri in the Museum and, above all, in his *Teaching of Amenemapt* which he completed in 1924.

The story of the series of strange dreams that marked the turning point in his life was told by Sir Wallis Budge to his close personal friend, Sir Henry Haggard, who included them in his book *The Days of My Life,* published in 1926. The publisher, J. C. Longman, included a special footnote stating that Sir E. A. W. Budge had seen and approved publication of the account—thus making it one of the most credible instances of its kind on record, personally endorsed by one of the great names of science.

⁞ ∽ჿ⌒⁞

AUTHOR'S NOTE: Recommended for additional reading is the astounding case of Dr. Herman Hilprecht, noted Assyriologist of the University of Pennsylvania, and the dream that enabled him to complete his book on *Old Babylonian Inscriptions*—after all other methods failed. See *Stranger Than Science,* page 51.

48

Louis Agassiz's Dream Discovery

One of the best loved scientists of his day was the brilliant and gentle Louis Agassiz, whose discoveries opened the door to a new epoch in his chosen field. He, too, must be listed among those who found their problems solved in their dreams.

Louis tells how he was baffled for weeks by the task of transferring the rather vague image of a fossil fish from the stony bed in which it had been preserved. He tried the conventional process without success. Then he improvised, also without success. Finally unable to figure out any new approaches, he simply gave up, put the fossil-bearing slab on the shelf, and went on to more promising assignments.

A few nights after he had decided to forget the matter he had a dream in which he seemed to see the entire fossilized fish as it had been in life. The impression on his mind was so strong that he again took down the vexatious slab to examine its image—but it was as vague as ever. Back to the shelf it went.

But the dream persisted. That night it returned and again he examined the fossil only to find it unchanged.

Hoping that he might have the same dream a third time, Agassiz placed a paper and pencil beside his bed. Sometime during the night his dream came back. Drowsy, in total darkness, he sat on the edge of the bed and traced out the clearly-outlined form of the prehistoric fish he had just seen in his dream.

Next morning he was surprised to see what he had drawn, and a little disappointed, for his drawing revealed detail which he had never before seen on the fossils and which he frankly held to be impossible. Taking the drawing with him as a guide, he went back to the slab and carefully chipped away at the stone on the off chance that it might actually contain more detail. To his delight he found that it did—for as a paper-thin layer of stone came loose there was the identical anatomical peculiarity he had drawn from his dream. Agassiz realized that the fossil looked fuzzy because it had not been completely uncovered, an error he hastened to correct.

When the imprint of the entire fish was exposed, it stood out in sharp relief, unique and hitherto unknown, and in every way exactly like the one in his dream drawing, which had shown him the fossil while it was still concealed beneath a layer of stone.

The experience impressed the noted scientist so strongly that Agassiz recounts it in his book, *Recherches sur les Poissons Fossiles.*

49

Human Blowtorch

It made headlines for a day in 1927 when a Vice President of the U.S., Charles Dawes, personally investigated the case of a man who reportedly had the uncanny knack of setting combustible material afire by simply breathing upon it. Dawes and his associates decided that there was no hoax involved, and since no logical explanation could be made, there the matter rested.

They might have been less reluctant to discuss the case had they known of its remarkable precedent. Dr. L. C. Woodman, of Paw Paw, Michigan, kept hearing of a young Negro who supposedly had to be very careful where he breathed to avoid setting unwanted fires. The doctor dismissed the rumors as nothing more than exaggerations until the day when A. W. Underwood, then twenty-four years old, walked into his office seeking help.

The astounded medic reported in the *Michigan Medical News* that, in the presence of himself and some of his colleagues, Underwood repeatedly performed some incredible feats. Doctor Woodman wrote:

"Underwood will take anybody's cotton handkerchief and hold it tightly against his mouth while breathing through it. After a few seconds it bursts into flames. The flames continue until the handkerchief is consumed. He will undress completely, rinse out his mouth thoroughly and submit to the most rigorous examination to preclude the possibility of any humbug. Yet his breath blown upon any paper or cloth envelops it in flames. He can collect dry leaves and start a fire by breathing on them."

The doctor noted that Underwood had to press the material against his mouth in such a manner that he could force his breath through it in order to shorten the process, whatever it was. The medics rinsed the man's mouth with various solutions, required him to wear surgeon's rubber gloves—but the phenomenon persisted.

This is a unique case, in that Underwood permitted himself to be subjected to investigation for months and, although the report was published in the *Michigan Medical News* and other similar publications, no one ever proposed any explanation of it.

50

The Face
That Returned

The American portrait painter, Girard Hale, is known everywhere for his magnificent head of Christ, which was one of his later compositions.

In 1928, while Hale was working in Paris, he was commissioned to do a portrait of a very wealthy Frenchwoman whose identity he never divulged because of the strange circumstances involved. He had never met either the lady or her husband. The commission stipulated that he was to paint the portrait at their home on the Loire.

In order to reach his destination, he had to take a train which would let him off at a small station. There were few passengers and he was alone in his own compartment. From boredom, perhaps, he dozed off, and when he awakened he discovered that a young lady now occupied the seat opposite his own. He noted that she was good looking but not beautiful, with a certain wistfulness that intrigued him.

For a while they exchanged trivialities, then she surprised him by changing the conversation to contemporary painting. She showed a surprising knowledge of his own work. Hale sought vainly to place her in his memory, for it seemed certain that she could not have known so much about him and his works unless he knew her . . . but he could recall no one who looked or talked like her.

"Could you paint me from memory?" she asked.

"Possibly," the painter replied, "but I would much prefer to paint you from life."

A few miles from Hale's station the train halted briefly at a tiny hamlet. The girl rose and bade him a friendly farewell. Hale was about to ask her name when she smiled and shook her head.

"We shall meet again before you have had time to forget me!" she said. Then she stepped out the door and was gone.

When he reached his station, Hale was warmly welcomed by his host and hostess, who proved to be quite elderly. They drove him to their chateau and left him to dress for dinner, which was timed for a couple of hours after his arrival.

As he made his way downstairs he was surprised to see a young lady—that same young lady with whom he had spoken on the train a few hours earlier. As she passed him, she smiled and said: "I told you that we would meet again!"

"Had I known you were coming here, too, perhaps we could have come by the same route."

Her smile faded.

"I'm afraid that would have been rather difficult!" Then she waved her hand as though to signify that she was in a hurry and ran on up the stairs.

At dinner, Hale made a casual reference to the young lady whom he had met, first on the train and again on the stairway. His host suddenly stiffened and glanced quickly at the hostess, who had stopped eating and was staring at her plate in silence.

"A young lady? In this house? I cannot imagine to whom you refer, young man. We have no young lady here nor are we expecting one."

Hale says that he began to describe the young lady and he noticed that both the host and hostess were quite disturbed, so he dropped the subject. It was not mentioned again during the meal but later, when the three of them were seated around the coffee table, the host broke a long silence.

"Please do me a great favor, Monsieur Hale—please sketch for me the face of the young lady whom you met on the stairs tonight!"

Fortunately he could recall vividly the face of his strange traveling companion and within a matter of a few minutes he had drawn an excellent likeness of her, endowing it with the smile she had worn as he approached her on the stairs. As he worked on the finishing touches, his hostess stepped beside him where she could see the sketch. She took one look and slumped to the floor in a faint.

After she had been revived, her husband sat beside her on the couch with his arm around her, and together they studied the sketch which Hale had made.

"We do not mean to be discourteous," said the host, "but many years ago we had a daughter, our only child, who died while we were on a trip to the orient. It must have been she whom you met on the train and again in this house tonight. This sketch you have drawn from memory, sir, is a perfect likeness of her!"

51

Case Of The Worried Wizard

The money was gone—every last dime of it. Old Mrs. Harmon got the first shock when she reached behind the eight-day clock on the shelf in the kitchen to add a few more dollars to the roll that had accumulated there.

That was only the beginning. She called her three spinster daughters and her son, John, and apprised them of what had happened. They all knew of the money, of course, since they had helped to save it from the proceeds of the farm. Their father, like his father before him, had been a frugal man. When he died in 1865, the family had continued to live on their fine two hundred and fifty acre farm in Monroe County, Indiana, and to save every dollar they could, just as they had seen him do. They had about four thousand dollars in paper money hidden in five places (each member of the family had a separate treasure-trove), and when their mother's savings vanished from behind the kitchen clock they scattered to check on their individual hide outs—to find all of them empty.

The stunned family sat down wordlessly in the kitchen to consider the enormity of the blow that had struck them. All were adults; all had complete confidence in the other members of the family. None were pranksters. None were thieves. None had any idea who could have taken the money.

After a long, pained silence, John took command. One by one he questioned his sisters, Rhoda, Rachel and Nancy. All had added to their individual holdings within the ten day period before the money vanished. Mrs. Harmon, too, had checked her funds about ten days before she discovered them missing.

As they carefully considered the circumstances under which the bills had been taken, it became apparent that whoever got the money had known exactly where to look in each instance and since nothing else in the house had been disturbed there was reason to suspect that the thief had been a member of their own little family group.

For several months they did nothing definitive about their missing money except worry. But little by little tempers grew short, hints were dropped and finally they began accusing each other. Poor old Mrs. Harmon could not believe that she had raised a thief of either sex but her efforts to still the arguments were futile. Inevitably, the family fight led to lawyers when two of the girls hired an attorney to investigate their brother and the other sister, who promptly retaliated by hiring themselves an attorney to clear their names.

The story got out, of course, and it was a much-discussed matter in and around Bloomington, Indiana, in 1880. There were plenty of theories, including one that John had a mistress in Indianapolis who had involved him in a blackmail scheme. Another rumor was that one of the spinster sisters had given the money to a secret lover who had failed to send for her, as promised. The public imagination, unfettered by facts, can produce a variety of fantastic rumors and so it proved in the Harmon case. The stories were interesting but groundless, as the opposing attorneys soon discovered.

Affairs had reached this Mexican stand-off in the summer of 1881 when a local newspaper reporter, D. O. Spencer, known as "Colonel" in the community, began giving exhibitions of what he called "mind reading" in various schools in south central Indiana. He was well known, likable, and his performances always drew good crowds. Actually, he was mixing a little hypnotism with some sleight-of-hand, and made no pretense of invoking any extra-mundane powers.

One night the Harmon family attended one of his performances in a school auditorium near their home and suddenly John was struck with an idea: could this man solve the mystery of the missing money? His mother and sisters agreed that it was worth a try and during a lull in the show John arose and asked his question.

It caught both performer and audience unawares and a dead silence fell over the auditorium while Spencer struggled for an answer.

"I don't know," he replied, with a nervous little giggle in his voice—"but I'll try it if you like."

The crowd burst into applause that gave the embattled mentalist a badly needed respite in which to think. He had never done anything like this before; might not be able to achieve anything except the dubious distinction of making an ass of himself. He had to turn it off, or at least twist it around from the success-or-failure that faced him.

"You understand, of course, Mr. Harmon, that the spirits do not work without pay? They always demand ten percent of what I find, if I find anything."

The crowd burst into laughter and the tension was eased. Spencer quickly explained that this would be something new for him—something purely experimental—and that he would go to the Harmon farm on the following day not for any share of the proceeds, if any, but merely to try to help this distressed family recover their property.

When Spencer's brightly-painted rig drew up at the scene of the experiment the next day, the house and yard were jammed with the curious, the skeptical and the smugly cynical. One estimate placed the crowd at three hundred and noted that it was a hot, sultry day and that the pump handle never stopped squeaking, even while Colonel Spencer was trying to solve the riddle.

Led by John, he made his way into the jam-packed sitting room, where Mrs. Harmon and her three daughters were nervously awaiting his arrival. Spencer explained that the crowd must be silent while he worked. He would, he said, hypnotize each member of the family in turn and ask them to lead him to the money. It might work, he pointed out, and it might not; at any rate he was willing to try if they were.

Nancy promptly broke into tears, so he passed her by.

Rachel was quickly hypnotized, but she responded like a log, so the Colonel had to discontinue the experiment with her. That left John, his mother and Rhoda; and the mentalist selected the girl. She quickly dropped into a trance at his suggestion. Spencer placed his hand against her forehead and said:

"You are now going to go straight to the place where the money is hidden. You will walk slowly, following me, straight to the hidden money. If I make a wrong turn you will stop. Now, walk to the money!"

By this time Spencer was soaked with sweat, for the crowded room was stifling hot. Walking slowly backward, with the girl's head pressing against his palm, he moved backward through the crowd. Once outside he started around the house and, before he had gone ten steps, Rhoda stopped. Spencer came back and replaced his hand, moving around her until her head again pressed against his palm.

Slowly, uncertainly, the strange couple began working their way toward the huge barn that stood about two hundred feet behind the house, but when Spencer tried to angle their course straight to the barn the girl stopped. He made several false starts without any cooperation from her until at last he spotted a corn crib built of logs about a hundred yards from the barn and off to one side.

When he began moving in that direction the pressure of the girl's head against his palm became more pronounced. By the time they were within fifty feet of the crib he could hardly restrain her. He started to enter the crib but Rhoda stopped. He moved toward the corner of the building and she forced him backward as fast as he could step. At the corner of the structure she stopped and refused to move in any direction.

Spencer mopped his brow, ordered the crowd back a few paces and called for a shovel. "Dig here, men. This is the spot! I believe we've got it!"

A few shovelfuls of earth were scooped from beneath the heavy logs that made up the corner of the crib and they uncovered a roll of tattered newspapers. Spencer grabbed them and peeled back the crumbly layers. There was the money, four rolls of greenbacks. Some of it had been badly chewed by rats—some of it had mildewed—some of it was in good condition—but it was all there!

In those days it was considered quite genteel for young ladies to faint, and Rhoda promptly obliged when the exuberant Spencer brought her out of her hypnotic sleep. But in her case there was considerable justification, with the heat, the excitement, and above all the sight of that missing money.

John Harmon carefully dumped the damaged bills into a flour sack and took it to Bloomington for deposit in the First National Bank.

And Colonel Spencer? He graciously refused to accept the percentage on behalf of his "spirits"—he had only been joking, he explained to anyone who asked, and after all, it was really Rhoda who had found the money, not he.

There was a bumper crop of theories about this amazing incident, of course, but Colonel Spencer may have been closest to the truth when he said that Rhoda evidently was a sleepwalker who gathered up the rolls of bills from their various hiding places and buried them where they were found, returning to her bed still asleep and without memory of her deed when she awakened. Under hypnosis, he theorized, her subconscious (he called it "unconscious") mind could retrace the steps to the hiding place.

Perhaps Spencer felt that he was tinkering with something that was too big for him and certainly something that he did not fully understand; or, again, perhaps he felt that he had reached his peak and that he should quit while he was on top. At any rate and for whatever reason, he dropped out of the mentalist field after the sensational Harmon case.

As the *Indianapolis News* commented on the case some years later: "After that, Mr. Spencer was known as somewhat of a wizard!"

52

The Strange Power Of Dreams

Lloyd Magruder never knew what struck him.

The moon was down and the lonely buttes along the Clearwater were faintly silhouetted against the sky. Magruder was a hundred miles from civilization, standing guard over the animals of his pack train. His several companions, with one exception, were rolled in their blankets around the embers of the campfire a hundred yards from Magruder. That one exception was a border ruffian named D. C. Lowry, who had left his blankets, alerted his fellow conspirators, James Romaine and David Howard, and sneaked, ax in hand, toward his unsuspecting victim.

As Magruder stood there in the darkness Lowry inched up within striking distance and swung his ax with terrible force. The impact embedded the weapon so deeply, in fact, the killer had to place his boot on the victim's chest and tug with all his might to free the heavy blade.

Silence was imperative, for four others in the little party around the campfire were also marked for murder. Lowry and his accomplices set about their bloody business and in a matter of seconds they had hacked to death the two young miners who had joined the pack train only the day before, and the Chalmers brothers, on their way from Missouri to Lewiston, Idaho to buy a mine.

The killers left their victims wrapped in their blankets and threw the bodies into a deep canyon nearby. They had searched the bodies, of course, and taken a total of about thirty-five thousand dollars in gold from them. This, with the rich loot from the heavily laden freight wagons, was a sizable fortune in October of 1864.

But one major problem remained, that of how to get away from the scene of the crime in that lonely spot along the Clearwater and how to get out of that part of the country undetected.

The killers reasoned that they would keep one good horse and seven mules for traveling and they drove the other animals off into the same canyon where they had dumped the bodies.

Their chances of escape looked good, for the murders had been arranged at a lonely spot that was a hundred miles from the nearest habitation and the victims had been dispatched in total darkness.

Unfortunately for them, the killers had reckoned without the strange power of dreams.

Back in Lewiston, Lloyd Magruder and Hill Beachy had become close friends when Magruder had been a regular customer at Beachy's Luna Hotel. And on the night of Magruder's murder Beachy had an alarming dream—in which he suddenly saw clearly the features of the ruffian who killed his friend with an ax—and saw him wrench the ax loose by putting his foot on the fallen man.

The dream was so vivid that Beachy told many of his friends about it.

Meanwhile, the killers had tried to cross the Clearwater at a point about fifty miles north of Lewiston. High water blocked their passage and they left their stolen pack animals with a rancher who was to keep them until called for, while they walked into the town.

The Walla Walla stage coach was due that day and when Lowry went into the Luna Hotel to buy tickets for the trio, Hill Beachy had the disquieting feeling that this was the man he had seen in the nightmare—the wielder of the ax that killed his good friend Magruder. But he was powerless to take action, for dreams make poor evidence in court and at that time there was no certainty that Magruder was not alive and well.

A few days after Lowry and his companions had left on the Walla Walla stage, Beachy heard about the pack animals they had abandoned at the ranch on the Clearwater. He and the sheriff hurried out there and discovered that in their haste, or carelessness, the killers had left Magruder's personal saddle and other items, including his revolver, among the gear. Beachy had himself deputized, swore out warrants for the arrest of Howard, Romaine and Lowry and got the necessary requisitions from the governors of Oregon, Washington and California.

He trailed the guilty trio to San Francisco and caught them while they were waiting for their stolen gold dust to be minted into coins. Brought back to the Idaho Territory, they were defendants in the first session of the District Court ever held in the Territory, a trial which began on January 5, 1865.

The chief witness against them was a fourth member of the gang, Bill Page, who had taken no part in the murder. He showed officers where the bodies had been dumped into the canyon. Examination showed that Magruder had been killed by one terrible blow from an ax, just as Beachy had seen it in his dream, even to the bloody footprint on the victim's thigh as he pried the ax from Magruder's body.

The accused were found guilty and Judge Samuel C. Parks sentenced them to death. Lowry, Howard and Romaine went to the gallows on March 4, 1865.

They had been captured and brought to justice because Hill Beachy recognized one of the trio as the killer he had seen in his dream.

53

Garroway's Missing Money

If you are one of those multitudes of persons who have had mystifying experiences involving dreams, then you travel in distinguished company. Among them is the famous TV star Dave Garroway, who knows what happened but he doesn't know to this day how or why.

In 1930, according to Mr. Garroway's own account of the puzzling experience, he was a high school student in his home town of University City, Missouri. A bunch of the boys were whooping it up with a dice game behind the high school one evening and Dave had what they call a hot run of the dice. He just couldn't lose.

As player after player dropped out, broke, Davie's winnings steadily mounted. Presently he had cleaned all the other players. Dave counted his winnings, $300.00, and stuffed the money into his pocket. When he arrived home he carefully tucked the money between the pages of a book called *The Gold Hunters,* which he happened to be reading at the time . . . and put the book on the top shelf in his closet.

Next morning he discovered to his dismay that the book and the money were both gone. Since his parents were away at the time Dave assumed that he must have misplaced the money, and he carefully searched the entire apartment, without results. It could not have been stolen for he had not left the room after hiding the three hundred dollars in the closet.

Several years later when Garroway was a student at Washington University in St. Louis, he told one of his professors of this strange experience. The teacher suggested that Garroway may unknowingly have moved the money himself, possibly while asleep. At the professor's suggestion, Garroway submitted to some hypnotic treatments and over a period of several weeks they patiently retraced his actions on the day he won the money.

Everything checked except for a period of about two hours on the night the money and the book vanished. They continued the hypnotic treatments in their efforts to unravel that missing two-hour period and it was during this series of treatments that Garroway awoke one morning to find the book and the money lying beside him in the bed.

Garroway's feet were black, the bedsheet streaked with dirt. While asleep, he had evidently recalled hiding the book and had gone after it and returned to his own bed . . . but when he did, he had to make the trip barefooted, in January.

54

Roger Williams
Was Delicious!

History books tell us that Roger Williams was a student at Cambridge before he came to the austere New World in 1631. He was banished from the Massachusetts colony for his outspoken views on religious freedom and made his way to what is now Rhode Island, where this first great champion of religious freedom in the New World served with distinction as leader of that colony.

Williams died in 1683, by which time he had become one of the most honored and beloved men of his time and state. He and his wife were buried side by side, on their farm, with a fitting, but by no means elaborate, headstone to mark their resting place.

When it was finally decided to erect a suitable memorial to Roger Williams, many years after his death, a commission was authorized to dig up the remains for more elaborate interment. Accordingly, the group opened the two graves—and found them empty. Roger Williams and his wife were gone. Not even their bones remained.

It was a most remarkable case of grave robbing, for the thief was actually caught in the act, although it required some time for the committee to recognize the culprit.

A short distance from the graves stood a robust apple tree, known widely for the fine quality of its fruit. The roots of the apple tree had penetrated the coffins of Roger Williams and his wife. A large root crept into the spot once occupied by our hero's head, where it made a turn, as if bypassing the head, and entered what had been the chest cavity, following the spine to the feet. At the feet the roots turned sharply upward, for the obvious reason.

These roots, which absorbed both of the Williamses by identical procedures, bore a remarkable resemblance to the human forms they had displaced. The main roots, with their multitudes of branches, resembled the circulatory system of the body. The evidence was so unmistakable that the roots were removed and preserved. They are still on deposit with the Rhode Island Historical Society.

Thus it became known that those who had long enjoyed the fine fruit from the tree in Roger Williams' graveyard had in fact been eating the noted historical figure. Through the alchemy of Nature, the hero had turned into apples.

55

Peter Hurkos —
The Man With
The Radar Brain

The date: October 3, 1961.

The big clock on the wall of the television studio stood at 8:50 p.m.—the program had just ten minutes left to run when Peter Hurkos sat down across the desk from me.

These ten minutes were to be the most startling in my more than thirty-five years of broadcasting.

I introduced Mr. Hurkos to the audience as a world-famed psychic, visiting Indianapolis as a guest speaker at a book promotion. He described briefly the accident that had led to his strange talent. He mentioned the long months in Buchenwald concentration camp, his former godlessness, and told how the acquisition of his mysterious gift had convinced him that he should use it for all people, of all races and religions.

At that moment I sprung my surprise.

I handed Mr. Hurkos a small notebook, a book that had once been the property of a young girl who had met a tragic end—the victim of a sex fiend who had never been caught. Hurkos did not know of this—and I did not tell him.

"Does this book mean anything to you, Mr. Hurkos?"
He frowned a bit and turned the book over slowly in
his left hand, without opening the book. Suddenly he gave
a start.

"Look!" he exclaimed. "Look at my hand!" He held out
his left hand. Sweat was pouring from it's palm. The other
hand was quite dry.

"She is dead!" Hurkos continued. He clutched his
throat. "She could not breathe—blood in the throat! He
grabbed her from the back when she tried to run from the
car—grabbed her and hit her behind the ear—here— (pointing to the left ear)—she fell down. He was afraid—he threw
her body into the deep ditch at the end of the bridge and
drove away. It was murder!"

Although there were thirty-four persons in the studio
at the moment, including guests and technicians, by this
time there was absolute silence as we awaited his next
remark. Hurkos sat hunched forward in his seat, staring
straight ahead into the dark behind the cameras, his finger
tips groping lightly over the note book. From the control
room overhead I could hear the faint hum of the video
tape machines that were recording the scene as it developed.

At length he spoke again.

"She lies dead in a ditch. It is not in the country—but
it is not in the city. They have come from the city in his
car. The body is in deep ditch—brush all around. There is
a bridge and only one house. Beyond the house the road
forks—maybe a quarter of a mile beyond the house. The
killer knows this place—he has been here many times
before. He is a man who—"

Suddenly Hurkos stopped.

"I will not say more—not here! This is murder! I see it. I want to talk to police!"

In exactly six thrill-studded minutes, Peter Hurkos had reconstructed the details of a brutal murder that had occurred at night on a lonely road slightly more than two years before. He had been correct in every detail of what he had said—and he had done it by simply fingering an object that had been the personal property of the victim.

The big question remained — could he identify the killer?

In a subsequent session with him, at which I was able to provide him with a garment taken from the body of the slain girl—he proceeded to describe in detail the events which he said led up to the ill-fated meeting of the girl and her killer. Hurkos named relatives of the man who is guilty of the crime (in his estimation). He described the establishment where the alleged killer works and described the man himself in such minute fashion that a subsequent check showed Hurkos to be correct, even to a minor blemish which detectives had not previously noted on the suspect's hand.

Of the three suspects who had been under scrutiny, Hurkos described and dismissed two, and urged that all attention be directed to securing a confession from the individual whom he fingered as the slayer.

The amount of detail in his statements is almost incredible. Hurkos described one wall of the victim's home, even to a picture on the wall and the fact that the person in the picture had a pronounced gap between the front teeth. He was absolutely correct on every statement he made where patient work had already checked on those points as evidence. Since his assertions regarding known facts were correct, there is reason to believe that he may also be correct about his charges naming as the killer a man who is still at large—but whose guilt remains to be proved. Hurkos says he is so confident that the man he describes actually killed the girl that he will gladly return to Indianapolis at his own expense to confront the suspect and charge him with the crime.

As I write this report, in late October of 1961, the matter rests at that point. The killer is still at large. The slaying is still unsolved. And Hurkos is still waiting for the call to face the man whom he accuses of the crime.

Peter Hurkos is a fantastic fellow, of course, as the well-authenticated records of his career clearly confirm. Today he lives in Milwaukee, happily married and with a substantial income assured, for Hurkos used his weird talents to locate for himself and a small group of associates the fabulous Lost Dutchman gold mine, in Arizona, one of the legendary treasures of the West.

Peter says he still does not understand his gift, but he is grateful for it and willing to share it, if sharing it benefits his fellow man.

The undeniable psychic talents with which Peter Hurkos is endowed have been put to good use by the police of many lands, enabling them in many cases to solve crimes previously considered beyond hope of solution.

Actually, it all began as the result of an accident when Hurkos was a prisoner of the Germans, working on a barracks building in June of 1943.

He was a house painter and was standing near the top of a thirty-six-foot ladder when his foot slipped and he fell to earth, fracturing his skull. He was rushed to The

Hague's famed Zuidwal Hospital, where he lay unconscious for three days. When he finally opened his eyes, Hurkos found himself lying in a bed next to one occupied by a patient named Aard Camberg, whom he had never seen nor heard of prior to that moment. For some reason which he never understood (and still doesn't) Hurkos turned to Camberg and said: "You're a bad man. Your father died recently and left you a gold watch but you have already sold it!"

The dumbfounded occupant of the next bed sat up and stared at Hurkos in amazement. "You are from Rotterdam and you have in your bag some money you stole from the place where you work," Hurkos continued.

With that, the target of his remarks bailed out of bed, scrambled into his clothes and rushed out past a nurse, who tried vainly to stop him. When Hurkos told her what had happened, she called a psychiatrist, Dr. Pieters, who promptly diagnosed it as a case of extrasensory perception. For the doctor's benefit, Hurkos told the nurse he saw her on a train and that she was about to lose a valise that belonged to a friend. The startled nurse said: "Doctor! I've just returned from Amsterdam and I forgot the valise in the dining car!"

For nine weeks Hurkos suffered from lack of sleep and violent headaches before the medics decided that he was out of danger as a result of the fall from the ladder. Physically he was restored to his former condition, but mentally he had entered a new and puzzling phase of his existence. Peter Hurkos would never be the same.

He found that something had happened to his brain which brought him a sense of confusion and uneasiness when he was in the presence of other people. He says he was deluged with mental images of their thoughts and fears.

About that time he found that, if he touched or handled objects which had been closely associated with other persons, he could frequently see those persons well enough to describe them and their whereabouts. With so many persons missing or displaced by the fortunes of the German invasion, he was frequently asked to locate missing friends and relatives who had been hustled away into Germany.

During the closing years of World War II, Hurkos was used by the Dutch underground forces to weed out counterspies who tried to infiltrate the movement. Since no records of such things were kept, it can only be said that Hurkos was constantly in demand and that one of the former underground officers, Gert Goosens, told newsmen after the war that Hurkos was "priceless and infallible!"

For our purposes it is more than adequate to deal with only a sampling of the widely-publicized cases on which Hurkos was used by police.

Sometimes his activities produce some surprising overtones, as when he was employed by a merchant of Roubaix, France, to help him locate a tin box containing about thirty thousand dollars worth of gold. The merchant had buried it in his garden at a time when the hoarding of gold was a crime. In 1951, after the ban had been lifted, the merchant went to dig up his treasure—and it was gone. He was inclined to believe that his business partner had stolen it but he dared not accuse him without some evidence. Hurkos agreed to try to locate the missing gold in return for twenty-five per cent of what he found.

He started his search at the vegetable garden where the anxious hoarder told him it had originally been buried.

He could detect no indication that the gold was buried anywhere in the garden, yet he told the owner that it *was* there, somewhere, so he kept crisscrossing the place, slowly working toward the small greenhouse. Finally he dashed into that structure, dumping plants out of their racks onto the ground while the gardner vainly tried to tear him away from his vandalism. When Hurkos upended one box that contained only earth and no plants, the missing box full of gold fell out.

The gardener admitted that he had found it accidentally while spading in the garden and that he and his father had secreted it temporarily in the greenhouse until such time as they could make off with it. The plotters each got six months in jail, the hoarder got his gold but Hurkos got cheated out of the share which had been promised him; after all, said the hoarder, they had no contract!

One of the strangest experiences Hurkos has undergone involved the 1948 disappearance of Viola Widegren in Helgum, Sweden. She was an apprentice nurse who vanished on a visit to the home of her father and stepmother. The alarm went out when the head nurse phoned Viola's father to inquire why the girl was not at work and the father told her that he had thrown Viola out of the house and knew nothing more about her.

Local authorities ran into a stone wall of nothingness and, when neighbors of the missing girl induced Hurkos to see what he could do, he received a chill welcome from the baffled gendarmes. However, the police did take him to the farm of Carl Widegren and, after less than three minutes there, Hurkos suddenly blanched and became ill.

"The girl is dead—murdered!" he told the police. "Get me out of here quickly."

After he regained his composure, Hurkos told the authorities that the girl's slayer was her father and that her body was buried under the house, near the foot of the main stairway.

Under the circumstances, the authorities could not get a warrant to dig up the basement floor because they did not have sufficient evidence. Only with Widegren's consent could the excavation be made. He sneeringly said he would give that consent for twenty thousand krona, which the public quickly subscribed. Faced with this, Widegren backed down and again refused to permit the authorities to dig . . . and the mystery of his daughter's disappearance is still unsolved.

Although he could easily have sued Hurkos for having publicly accused him of murder, Widegren never did. Perhaps he was more than content to leave bad enough alone.

Peter Hurkos has upon many occasions submitted himself to lengthy testing by eminent specialists, including Dr. Rene Dellaerts, neurologist of the University of Louvain, who used an encephalograph to record Hurkos' brain reactions as the subject thumbed through a stack of photographs of individuals, about half of whom were dead. When Hurkos glanced at the pictures of someone who was dead his brain waves registered wide fluctuations, said Dr. Dellaerts. The noted specialist could only ascribe it to telepathic tendencies in a pronounced degree.

Peter van der Hurk of Dordrecht, better known as Peter Hurkos, was front-page copy for European newspapers for many years during which he was often called in to help baffled authorities solve all sorts of crimes. In all fairness it should be noted that he was not infallible nor did he pretend to be. It is also a matter of record that his rate of successes was so high that he was in constant demand. In addition to these tasks he also served (and still does) as consultant to several large industries in Europe, where his uncanny abilities have saved them both trouble and money.

The Belk Psychological Research Foundation brought Peter Hurkos and his wife to the United States in 1957 so that he would be available for study by specialists. For more than a year the famed Dutch psychometrist underwent examination and testing at Rockland, Maine, under the direction of Dr. André Puharich. Among other things, Hurkos was enclosed in a metal cage which was entirely surrounded by wires carrying high voltage. The purpose was to determine, if possible, whether a powerful magnetic field in any way affected his powers. Dr. Puharich came to the conclusion that it did not.

After the conclusion of the New England experiments, Hurkos was moved to Miami where he was sponsored on a television show, Mind Mysteries, over Channel 10, and where he also helped the Miami Police Department, upon invitation. It was while he was thus engaged that he stepped into the front pages of the nation's newspapers.

The Carroll Jackson family of Apple Grove, Virginia, vanished from their automobile on a rural highway in January of 1959. Two months later the bodies of the father and his infant son were found in a brush pile near Fredericksburg, Virginia. They had been shot to death. And on March 22, 1959, the bodies of the missing mother and her six-year-old daughter were found in the woods near Annapolis. They had been brutally ravished and murdered.

One of the most intensive manhunts in years produced

nothing but frustration. The FBI questioned and released more than a thousand suspects; the state and local police had much the same experience. The case seemed to be at dead end.

In June of 1960, Dr. Francis Riesenman, a psychiatrist at St. Elizabeth's Hospital in Washington, D.C., offered to pay Hurkos one hundred dollars per day and expenses if he would try to solve the murders of the Jackson family, who had been neighbors of Dr. Riesenman.

When Hurkos arrived, he was met by Virginia state and local police. He was given a shirt taken from the body of the slain man, and he soon began describing the killer— a dirty, drunken, bristly-haired fellow who dealt in garbage or something comparable. Hurkos named the brand of cigarettes the man smoked. The killer, he said, lived in a faded two-toned house and he specified the colors . . . and in the front yard, beside the door, Hurkos said he saw a broken chair—a straight-back chair—lying on its side.

It didn't take the local police very long to figure out a likely suspect. He was a well known local character who drove a junk truck. They descended on his house—which was exactly as Hurkos had described it, even to the broken chair lying in the yard. And the man's wife was also exactly as Hurkos had pictured her, even to the two missing front teeth which she said her husband had knocked out in a drunken fit.

The man was placed in custody. He had been missing from his home on the day the Jacksons vanished and he could not account for his activities. Dr. Riesenman suggested a sanity hearing for the suspect. It was held at the somewhat unusual hour of 1:45 a.m. and the suspect was hustled off to a state mental hospital after two doctors and the Judge found him insane. It was later explained that the doctors felt that the suspect might recover sufficiently after ninety days of treatment to be able to answer questions intelligently. The commitment was made at the technical request of the man's wife and he was never charged with the crime.

Hurkos had merely handled the victim's shirt and from it he described a man, his wife and their home so vividly that police had no difficulty finding them. That the man was eventually released is a matter of record, for another suspect was later picked up and sentenced for the crimes which Hurkos attributed to the suspect we have discussed. Hurkos contends that the wrong man was convicted and there is a chance that he may be right; for the young man who was eventually sent to prison for the Jackson murders was a sexual psychopath who was of dubious value as a witness.

Hurkos had named one man; the law had convicted another for the same offenses. So far as the law is concerned the matter is closed but Hurkos told newsmen in early 1961 that he is still convinced that the wrong man was convicted. On the basis of the past performance of this remarkable fellow he may very well be right. And if events bear him out by subsequently turning up the suspect whom he had named, Hurkos would be surprised least of all, for it would simply be another in a long list of cases on several continents where he had somehow known the answer all the time.

Internationally known as the result of this remarkable talent, Peter Hurkos is unquestionably one of the strangest of strange people.